THE NASSAU COLISEUM, NASSAU COUNTY, N.Y., OCTOBER 9, 1972:

Elton John sat alone in his white-tiled dressing room deep in the bowels of the giant sports arena like a lost little boy. Quiet, subdued, and calm. Tidy.

Suddenly he started to effect his transformation. He slipped from his well-tailored suedes into a nifty silver lamé number. He fastened his white winged boots and ran his fingers through his hair, cut short for the tour. His approach to the stage was amazing. It was almost like watching Dr. Jekyll drink the potion and turn into some outrageous beast...

Suddenly the stage is bathed in hot lights as the band pours and surrounds the pounding piano man as he belts out the lyrics that have made him a superstar. The audience starts dancing in their seats; they begin to boogie in the aisles. They scream, they swoon and faint...

There's a grin across Elton's face. The standing-room-only crowd is caught – hook, line, and sinker.

Cathi Stein

Elton John

Futura Publications Limited

A Futura Book

First published in Great Britain in 1975
by Futura Publications Limited

Copyright © Gerald Rothberg Publications Inc.

This book is sold subject to the condition
that it shall not, by way of trade or
otherwise, be lent, re-sold, hired out or
otherwise circulated without the publisher's
prior consent in any form of binding or
cover other than that in which it is
published and without a similar condition
including this condition being imposed on the
subsequent purchaser.

ISBN 0 8600 72010

Printed in Great Britain by
Hazell Watson & Viney Ltd,
Aylesbury, Bucks

CHRONOLOGY

1947	Reginald Dwight is born on March 25 in Pinner, Middlesex.
1950	Reg Dwight starts playing the piano by ear.
1951	Reg begins to play for his parents and friends on social occasions.
1956	Rock 'n' Roll breaks loose in Great Britain with Bill Haley's 'Rock Around the Clock'; Reg Dwight's mother buys the discs 'Hound Dog' and 'Heartbreak Hotel' by Elvis Presley.
1957	Reg takes private piano lessons. His parents divorce.
1959	Receives part-time scholarship to the Royal Academy of Music, located at York Gate, Marylebone Road, London.
	Enrolled at Harrow School in Pinner.
1960	Regs plays piano at Northwood Hills Inn, and later, buys an electric piano.
1961	Forms Bluesology with Harrow friends, Mick Inkpen, Stuart Brown, and Rex Bishop.
1963	Reg works part-time as a 'tea boy' at Mills Music in London. Does session work on cheap 'cover' recordings.
1965	Bluesology goes professional.
	Reg quits school after finishing his A-levels. Bluesology goes on Continental tour.
1967	Long John Baldry takes over the reins of Bluesology.

1968	Regs auditions at Liberty Music and meets Bernie Taupin.
1969	Reg changes his name to Elton John, records with Bernie, and releases *Empty Sky*.
1970	Records *Elton John*, and *Tumbleweed Connection*, makes two tours of the U.S.
1971	Releases *11-17-70*, *Friends*, and *Madman Across the Water*.
1972	Releases *Honky Chateau*, goes on the 'Legs Larry' U.S. tour.
1973	Releases *Don't Shoot Me. – I'm Only the Piano Player*. Makes another sell-out U.S. tour. Names Surrey estate Chez Hercules. Forms Rocket Records.
1974	Releases *Goodbye Yellow Brick Road*. Records at Caribou Ranch in Colorado. Tours Japan, Australia, Indochina, and Hong Kong.
1974	Releases *Caribou* and *Greatest Hits*.

CHAPTER 1

Seventeen thousand five hundred tickets sold in ninety minutes.

Humming along at triple speed, the mighty computers of Ticketron were nestled in a temperature-controlled chamber deep in the heart of Hackensack, New Jersey. The seats ticked off relentlessly, three per second. In five hundred lines at five hundred Ticketrons stretched from Montreal to Miami, from Pittsburgh to Bangor, the fans were lined up. The lines moved slowly toward the men, lit up like gray neon robots behind the green glass. Hands flew across computer consoles. The ticket buyers were impatient, calm, jumpy and quiet – all waited to come before the glass window. 'Two tickets, please,' demanded an excited youth in tattered jeans, while his girlfriend hugged his arm.

Hours of waiting fed fuel to their hopes, hopes which were being transformed into electronic blips the instant the youths laid their money across the counter. Conversation ran up and down the lines like a breeze.

'I think he's fantastic,' declared a clean-cut boy wearing a Peter Pan T-shirt. 'I've been a fan of his since he first came out. When he came to the Fillmore East in 1970, I was there the first night. I was there! I followed him to Chicago. He was so great I went back the next night.' The young man's excitement mounted. 'And I'm twenty years old. Maybe I should be out of the teenage idol stage, but I just happen to love the man's music.'

'I know what you mean,' agreed a girl in bare feet. 'I just can't stay away.'

The time was spring, 1972, and Elton John was in the middle of a gigantic marathon tour of the United States: forty-five concerts in about as many days. All the dates were sold out, not one seat left vacant.

On October 9, 1972, Elton John was scheduled to play the Nassau Coliseum, one of the largest and most important venues on his schedule. Waiting breathlessly for his performance were 17,500 fans. His tour had already been in progress for forty performances and from the outside looking in, the Elton John caravan appeared calm and organized. Inside, a whirlwind of activity was sweeping up the entourage into a white-ball of energy. To launch the elfin piano thumper on his enormous campaign, feats of heroic effort had to be displayed.

On the twelfth floor of a red-carpeted motel called the City Squire Inn, a costumer began to make a last-minute check on the racks of glittering outfits Elton would don during the careening course of the night's performance. She looked closely at the seams. Elton had a way of ripping his pants when he got going full steam, and seams had to be double and triple stitched. No bared jockey shorts that night.

The costumer pulled out a silver lamé suit with blue and red stripes. On top of it she laid out Elton's enormous orange-tilted fish-eye glasses and the short white boots with the little wings attached to the heels. 'Some of these costumes,' remarked a journalist who had visited the City Squire chambers that day, 'look like they were made by somebody's mother. Like she scraped together all the thrown-away tinfoil scraps she could find and the chocolate wrappers and made him a costume for the annual kindergarten play.' Under transforming kleig lights they would glitter and glow like the garments of a magic king himself, spun from the webs of a million bewitched silkworms and dazzled fields of spiders.

Next to Elton's costumes hung the wild getups of his crazy tap-dancing friend, Larry Smith. 'Legs' Larry had been tapping his heels and clicking his toes across America for the entire tour. His room was a jungle of clothes, arms, feet, with Legs Larry sitting in the middle of it all. 'They were screaming for me, dear child,' he said of the American audiences, jumping and twitching his way across the floor to the blaring TV set to turn the volume up a notch. 'Screaming for little old Bonzo Larry. It's unbelievable. It's incredible.'

Larry, one of England's freakiest rockers from the early sixties, paced back to the TV set on top of which stood a collection of plastic soccer players in 4-2-4 formation. Close to them stood a photograph of Doris Day, as she appeared in *Love Me or Leave Me*, with a toothy smile on her face, the one that makes you glow with happiness when you look at her.

Larry had been the lead singer with the now defunct Bonzo Dog Doo Dah band. And he had first met Elton John when he made a cameo appearance on Elton's *Honky Chateau* album, tap-dancing on the 'Killing Myself' track. Elton and Larry hit it off back then like a house afire and when the U.S. tour came up, the piano man invited Legs to come along.

'That's how it was,' said the young reporter at the City Squire Inn. 'Larry was so excited about going on the road with Elton he quickly designed ten outfits in one day and had them made up by a London tailor the very next day. Then he called Elton and said, "I'm ready! When are we off?" '

While everybody else was preparing for the ride out to the Nassau Coliseum, Larry was busy too. He was bending over the sort of plastic bride and groom that usually adorned a towering, white wedding cake. But Larry was gluing the pair to the top of a silver crash helmet, the kind worn by cooled-out hot-rod chopper daddies when they want to make a big splash on the drag run. Next he attached a wedding veil with white tulle and lacy edges to the crash helmet. On the hanger a white jump suit with padded shoulders hung behind short pants and a tiny colorful vest made out of exotic shiny material. There was also a mysterious-looking Parisian mackintosh, just like the ones spies wear in European intrigue movies.

The roadies' chartered bus took off for the Nassau Coliseum at high noon. The bus embarked from the caravan's temporary den at the brick-and-plastic City Squire Inn on the corner of Seventh Avenue and Fifty-first Street near the seedy Times Square area of Manhattan. The roadies whistled at street women and leered at porno-movie titles and weird pleasure shops along the way.

Following the roadies' bus, Elton's equipment trailer wended its way through the teeming vehicles trying to escape from the brainlike density of the huge metropolis.

Weekend traffic, exhaust fumes, honking horns, whizzing hot rodders jostled with the speeding vans. The driver held his breath as a dump truck lurched dangerously close to the left side of the equipment truck. Inside, its precious load of drums, guitars, mikes, amplifiers, monitors, and lighting devices trembled with the shock absorbers. Slowly, the towering apartment buildings gave way to dark-red brick factories with signs on the sides saying, 'Isaac Bernstein, Shoe Laces and Button Holing Devices,' or 'Worldwide Pressing Co.' It was a new and totally baffling world to even the well-traveled roadmen.

The factories were superseded by rows of houses. Trees shot by in the hazy sunlight, then more factories. More and larger houses passed, followed by open space. Nothing ahead but the speeding trails of cars and trucks, road signs and grass. The land got even flatter. The Elton John caravan rolled on.

Suddenly, looming ahead and caught in the sunlight, rising up out of a mammoth parking lot, was a huge flying saucer of a building, a marshmallow made for an Atlas to toast over the bonfire of the sun. It was Nassau Coliseum, one of the largest auditoriums in the world.

The invaders from Great Britain, however, were undaunted by this heap of American architectural fantasy, and they drove through the miles of empty parking lot and down a long ramp into the very heart of the Coliseum.

Then the team of British and American roadies set to work hauling the tons of musical enhancers out of the truck and onto the awesome stage. That night the equipment would channel the rock 'n' roll sounds of the thundering piano men out into the cavernous hall over the heads of thousands. At this moment, though, the dome was empty, and only the rows of chairs bore witness to the performance of the road team.

First, the speakers were lifted out of the trucks. They were floated into place on the scaffoldings at either side of the stage by forklifts and by hand. Up on the stage right next to an organ sat Elton's mammoth grand piano. Nigel Olsson's drum kit was rushed up on risers to center stage, and pushed to the back. Davey Johnstone's amps and Dee Murray's monitors were placed at stage left next to a series of light boxes.

By 5:30 P.M. a bank of twelve-inch speakers were also in place, slightly fanned out for dispersal of maximum treble sounds. On top sat a grouping of five-inch speakers, tweeters, and more woofers and speakers of assorted sizes. The light console was set halfway back on the right-hand side. The sound mixers, manned by the famous Clair brothers, were located in the middle of the huge hall. Monitors were strategically placed around the stage. These speakers would enable Elton, Dee, Davey, and Nigel to hear what they were playing. Next came the puzzle of tracing the miles of coiled electrical cables from the amplifiers to the speakers. This took another two hours.

In a few hours Elton himself would be arriving for a sound check. The crew hurried as they climbed up the towers like ants, tightening wires, probing at grids, switching tiny knobs, twisting miniature screw-drivers, and hammering gently at stubborn tacks. Workmen yelled across the stadium to each other for assistance.

By 6:00 P.M. everything was all set up, at least well enough for Elton to make a sound check. The union men broomed down the floors. Unknown to no one, a few adventurous Elton fans were hiding in the back, having sneaked into the hall to listen to the sound check and camp out till the opening fireworks of golden light and chords.

The City Squire hotel phones began to ring as road managers tried to get everyone to the bus. Suddenly the cry echoed through the posh and plastic rooms, and everyone began to scurry around, remembering all the details so important to the glorious two hours ahead. Larry lifted up the Doris Day photo and the wedding-cake couple on the helmet, and with great care carried them to the waiting elevator, down, and into the late-afternoon air. The Greyhound gobbled him up and wended its way through the city toward Long Island.

Its seats were occupied by twenty-four quiet, well-tailored ladies and gentlemen. As he stumbled down the aisle to his seat, Legs Larry noted the familiar faces on the bus: Bernie Taupin and his tiny new wife, Maxine, Marvin Tabolsky, road manager for the U.S. juggernaut and producer Gus Dudgeon. Dee Murray cradled his bass on his knees while Nigel Olsson gazed up at the skyscrapers. Davey Johnstone, the razor-sharp guitarist who had just been added to the group, whisked imaginary lint off his lapels. Legs Larry clowned and mugged at all the passing traffic.

The bus lurched into a pothole on Third Avenue and smashed into the back of a parked Ford. The incident caused such a skirmish in the bus that it was later reported in all the underground papers. Then the bus chugged back into gear to join a two-mile-an-hour traffic jam.

Sitting alone in the back of the bus, a blond young man paid no attention to the jolts and bounces. Dressed from head to toe in buckskin, he crooned to himself. He was a neat-looking person. A tidy little man. Tidy hair, a tidy kind of face, tidy clothes, and a tidy thing or two to say to his friends as they crawled over the bumping, lurching floor of the bus to wish him luck. If he were any more compact a person, he'd be flat as a pancake, but there was a strange strength glowing around him, a kind of gentle charisma radiating from him all the time.

He gazed out of the bus window and spotted the Nassau Coliseum just as the huge golden sun sank behind the arena's vast bulk like an orange into a teacup. The bus shot a ramp, was swallowed by the mammoth Coliseum and entered its winding corridors. Larry exited the bus, still gingerly lifting his wedding cake helmet. Elton continued singing aimless tunes to himself as he walked down the empty halls.

Elton John sat alone in his white-tiled dressing room deep in the bowels of the giant sports arena like a lost little boy. Quiet, subdued, and calm. Tidy. Hidden inside his stubby body, caged and waiting until the magic spotlight moment, raged the happy monster of show biz, the piano-pounding boogie-bouncing animal who was literally ready to burst at the seams with energy.

Elton started to effect his transformation. He slipped from his well-tailored suedes into a nifty silver lamé number. He fastened his white winged boots and ran his fingers through his hair, cut short for the tour. He didn't betray a flutter of nerves or a twitch of anxiety. In the dressing room everything was moonscape quiet for the countdown.

Things were very different not far down the bending corridor where the warm-up band, Family, stalked the hallways to the stage entrance. As they climbed up on top of the massive stage and their eyes turned toward the vastness of the Coliseum, there was only a ripple of applause from the crowds now massing and mingling about with quiet, excited energy. People seemed less interested in them than in exploring the new territory of the Coliseum, amazed at finding old friends in the tangled hive of dungareed, smoking, and scratching humanity.

Elton John's approach to the stage was amazing. It was almost like watching Dr. Jekyll drink the potion and, in several phases, turn into some outrageous beast. As he strode along the corridor, the mild, tidy character grew steadily from his stubby five feet, eight inches in platforms into a giant of glitter and power, neon lit with anticipation.

Elton strode on stage along, in his big platforms, dressed in his shimmering lamé suit with the blue and white and red stripes, a pudgy fudge-ripple-ice-cream-sundae Uncle Sam. The deafening applause from 17,500 clappers greeted him like a tidal wave of love. He grinned with all his square little baby teeth showing and waved back to the audience. Bernie Taupin peeked from the shadowed wings, looking like a timid brown-eyed twin of the glittering kid on the stage.

As the mammoth house lights dim, a piercing spotlight picks out a lonely figure on stage. He walks across the stage alone, a chubby little body in tall platform shoes. He shimmers iridescently in his red, white, and blue lamé suit. The little figure quietly moves toward the black grand piano that looms on the stage like a crouching beast. The glittering man sits down, lifts his fingers over the keyboard, hesitates for one fraction of a second, then down come the fingers on the keys. The hall fills with the resounding chords of 'Tiny Dancer' as the crowd rises in a tidal wave of love.

Suddenly the stage is bathed in hot lights as the band pours out and surrounds the pounding piano man as he belts out the lyrics that have made him a superstar. The audience starts dancing in their seats; they begin to boogie in the aisles. They scream, they swoon and faint. Elton's stomping form is bathed in silver light, while blue, yellow, and red lights play over the rest of the stage, decorating Dee, Davey, and Nigel with shifting haloes of color.

Blue jean baby, L.A. lady, she's the seamstress of the band ...

Pretty-eyed, pirate smile, you'll marry a music man ...

From the tips of his locks to the toes of his winged high heels to the husky tones of his voice, Elton John, silver-suited hero, has captured the audience from his first note. The band is now cruising along, kicking up a storm, then laying down a swelling ocean for Elton to sail upon. Suddenly, halfway through 'Killing Myself' Elton lurches into some funky lyrical phrasing and Legs Larry Smith bursts out on stage, his grasshopper body all awiggle, waving his arms and miming, 'Gosh ... ah, gosh ... oh, golly.'

The entire auditorium erupts then, as Elton pushes back the piano stool and tap dances to a honky rush of 'Singin' in the Rain.' Elton and Larry prance across the stage dressed in Parisian slickers, while a girl whose body is painted in flowers strews handfuls of glitter upon them in a rainfall of gold. They stroll, they highstep. They rave.

Nigel Olsson blams away with a crisscross drum motion. The incredible Davey Johnstone rocks on his guitar while Dee thumps a startling bass. Elton stumbles back to his piano to race into 'Country Comfort.' Then 'Salvation' and 'Hercules.' Elton Hercules John. Long live the king, the biggest superstar in the world. There's a grin across his face, his silver trousers are hitched up to his knees, and his winged shoes shoot off into the air with every kick. The standing-room-only crowd is caught hook, line, and sinker.

CHAPTER 2

In the winter of 1947 Mrs. Sheila Dwight was very pregnant. But that was no deterrent to nature, which locked the island kingdom of Great Britain in the icy grip of the deadliest snow in seventy years. Already torn by the bombs and violent trials of World War Two, England was barely pulling through this new attack, launched by the gods themselves.

With the coming of March, Mrs. Dwight knew her child would be born any moment. As if impatient for the occasion, spring arrived early. The sun shone and commanded the frozen mountains of snow to melt. Steady streams of water poured from the banks of ice, running in rivulets down the streets into the drains of the cities, rushing into the farmland creeks with ever-increasing urgency. Newspaper headlines everywhere screamed with tidings of floods and death across the country.

Driving through the open land around Pinner, Middlesex, Mrs. Dwight could see the fields of crops turned into giant lakes of semifrozen water. Potatoes had begun to rot and the winter wheat had died on its stalks. Thousands of acres of precious food were lost. People were packing up their belongings and heading for the high country.

Mrs. Dwight feared for her unborn child as she heard that forty thousand acres of Britain's richest farmland was under water. And the Dutch, the dike experts of the world, had to be called in to advise about the desperate emergency measures which had to be taken.

While hardy Hollanders were working in the devastated countryside, the river Thames itself was flooding its banks in London, causing the worst traffic jam in the history of the capital. Two of the six subways stopped completely as water poured into the tunnels and debris from the flood clogged the filters through which the Thames water flowed as it cooled the city's heating systems and electrical plants. Just as Britain had struggled forward to restore some semblance of order to its war-torn economy, the natural catastrophe served with almost diabolical perversity to flatten the nation for years to come.

It was during this near emergency that Reginald Kenneth Dwight was born on a flood-ridden Tuesday – March 25, 1947 – a day during which his mother wasn't even sure the doctor would be able to get through the rising waters in time to minister to her labor.

If life had been arduous while Sheila Dwight was pregnant, it was almost impossible the first year of baby Reggie's life. The wild floods had wiped out the last remaining stores of food, and it was a battle for many English women to scrape together enough for each meal.

Although his homeland's economy was in catastrophic shape, Reggie Dwight's childhood was, perhaps, more comfortable than that of most. He lived in Pinner, Middlesex, a suburb situated on the rural edge of London. When Reggie was a child, London had not yet eaten into the Harrow countryside of which Pinner was a small township. There were still some ancient houses with thatched roofs, cobble-winding streets, and some pubs whose smoke-darkened walls and quaint windowsills dated as far back as the fifteenth century. Pinner was generally thought to be a 'good' neighborhood, far from the factories and belching refineries of many London areas.

In some places in London in 1947 a mother had to bundle her tiny son in woolens to keep out the cold. She would have to walk down the streets of row houses that had been flattened by the Germans' terror-filled assaults. The remains of a tin roof might flap eerily in the wind where once a house had stood. Even though the war had ended twenty-four months before, suspended time-release bombs lodged in the crannies of buildings would occasionally detonate in the night, and structures would be reduced to nothing in a matter of seconds.

In her neighborhood, Mrs. Dwight could avoid many of these hazards but, like everyone else, she had to queue up. Queues were unavoidable in postwar England. Mrs. Dwight stood in line for hours with her neighbors. Queuing had become a way of life, and she accepted the fact that it was going to be a long time until things changed. She probably accepted the fact that she lived in an abnormal world where most of her waking moments were spent standing on line. Britishers waited on line for everything: for food rations (bacon, bread, eggs, butter, and tiny portions of beef and milk), for fun, clothing, travel tickets, and petrol for their little cars. They stood in line for all of life's necessities.

The hottest-selling disc in Britain in 1950, when Reggie was three, was 'His Majesty's Voice,' the recorded mumblings of the ailing King George VI. It was all the English had to remind them of the Empire and past greatness. There were few treats for kids when Reggie Dwight was growing up. No toy trains, stuffed animals, or elaborately illustrated books. No TV either. What did Reggie do on long, cold winter days? He listened to the radio. And he went to the cinema with his mother to see Doris Day movies. He saw her in *Love Me or Leave Me* long before he could understand what a 'torch singer' was, or could know there was anything special about the era they called the thirties.

It was music that thrilled Reggie, and there was plenty of it in the house. The tall, statuesque Mrs. Dwight loved music, and every chance she got she bought a record to play on the old phonograph. She picked show tunes, music hall, dance jigs, and especially the American crooners. She turned on the BBC when she was cooking, cleaning, or doing the ironing and sang along to the melodies slipping along the airways. There wasn't much else to do.

Suddenly when Reggie was only three years old, he waddled over to the King Brothers upright and braced his wobbly little body against the piano. Then, to the amazement of his parents, he began to plunk out the melody of 'Skater's Walz' and a series of Top Ten songs. Sheila might have looked at Mr. Dwight in amazement. 'Where did Reg get such a gift?' she might have wondered. 'I didn't have any musical background,' she mulled later. 'My father, Reg's grandfather, had been involved in military music.' Maybe it was inherited.

Whenever the child threw a tantrum, his father discovered that the perfect cure was to set him in front of the King Brothers. Soon he might be banging away, his squeaky wail peeping out the lyrics to Eddie Fisher's 'Wish You Were Here,' or Winifred Atwell's rendition of 'Night and Day,' the Cole Porter hit.

Reg Dwight's musical career was furthered when he began to listen to his mother's records. Coming home from her job in the government offices, Mrs. Dwight would not be able to resist stopping and picking out the latest hit single. Reg climbed up on a chair and gingerly lifted the heavy disc with the colorful label on it and set it down on the turntable. He watched the tubes in the back of the record player slowly light up like tiny planets rising in the sky. He picked up the arm and set the needle gently on the record.

Out of the speakers leaped the voice of Kay Starr, moaning 'Fool, Fool, Fool,' Buddy Morrow, or Tennessee Ernie Ford booming 'Sixteen Tons.' Picture, if you will, Reg bobbing back and forth, watching the brilliantly colored labels spin round and round. He would be mesmerized. It would seem as if the labels were turning faster and faster – 78, 78, 78, 78, 78. They spun him off into a fantasy world of sounds, colors, visions. He liked the bright discs the best. Anything on London or EMI was boring because of those plain labels. His favorites were the ones with the funny stickers, especially the ones called Polydor.

As soon as the final notes evaporated into thin air, Reg was at the piano picking out the phrasing and chord structure. 'I didn't have any formal training,' Reg revealed later. 'I just sat down at the piano and could play. I started picking out the tunes, and it went like that for about three years.'

Even before Reggie was old enough to go to school his skill at the keyboard was put to use. Everytime there was a wedding reception, birthday party, or celebration of any kind, it was the same story. Sometimes his parents would take him with them when they went to visit, and Reggie would play a few numbers on the host's piano and then retire to the nursery. He always knew when such an evening was scheduled because he'd have to go indoors early in the afternoon.

One Friday in the late spring Reggie's mother might have called him in to bed. He would have protested, of course. It was still daylight and the other children were engrossed in a soccer skirmish. Why should he have to go in to bed? She might have explained: 'We're expecting a few guests tonight and we want you to come down later and play a few tunes. You know how much it means to your father and me – and the guests.'

Reggie loved to play the piano, but he absolutely detested command performances. Especially in front of strange people. 'I don't like people forcing me into playing,' he complained. Nevertheless, he went indoors, had tea and milk and a toasted scone, and went to his room. Soon he fell into a deep sleep.

'Wake up. Wake up, Reggie,' she could have said. 'Reginald, it's time to get up.' His mother's voice was kind, but insistent. It was warm and dark under the eiderdown quilts. Reg had been dreaming about faraway, dancing, brilliant colors. It was hard to tear himself away from the colors and pull himself out of the bed; but his moment in the spotlight had arrived.

A scene such as this might have occurred: Reg slowly crawling out of the covers, washing the sleep out of his eyes and getting dressed. From downstairs he could hear the sounds from the party. Ladies' high giggles were punctuated by the grunts and guffaws of the gentlemen. The clink of silverware against china rang in his sleepy head. Reg walked into the light of the living parlor. There, up against the textured wallpaper, was the upright piano.

Without any ado, Reg slipped behind the bench. The old polished wood of the instrument gleamed in the candlelight. He stared for a moment at the logo inscribed in ornate bold print on the front of the piano: 'King Brothers of London.' It seemed like a magical name.

The guests might have cheered him on. 'Oh, how darling. What a cute lad.' 'Isn't it marvelous that Sheila's son is so talented?' 'There's nothing more charming than a musical child.' 'He'll be headed for the Academy, eh what? Formal lessons soon?'

Slowly, Reggie would carefully place his little fingers on the ivory keys. The sharps and flats created a design as they jutted in between his fat pinkies.

The shy youngster sat with his back to the men and women, and he burned with the desire to get up and run. He hated being made to play before this crowd, yet his love of the piano and the sound of the rich notes reverberating around the room made him stay. He resented this intrusion on his private world of melodies, but he plunked his fingers down and the tunes flowed out around him. The well-groomed couples settled back in their chairs, and the tension which had been mounting since Reggie first sat down melted away. The adults began to nod their heads and tap their feet to the tunes.

The little boy played smoothly. He launched into a popular Frank Sinatra number, then a Dean Martin medley. Next came Frankie Laine's 'I Let Her Go Where the Winds Go,' and Jo Stafford's 'Diamonds Are a Girl's Best Friend.' Then he moved into Patti Page's 'Butterflies,' and a song which his mother liked (even though the newspapers booed it, as she had told him) called 'New Guitar Boogie Shuffle,' and its B-side 'The Sheik of

Araby.' The little boy played on heedless of the grown-ups and their pressures and his previous drowsiness. The baby piano man played tune after tune into the warm evening, a big grin on his round face.

CHAPTER 3

In 1954 Reg was seven years old, and the musical phenomenon sweeping the country was called Rhythm and Blues. Reg was enthralled by the R&B sounds, called 'race' records by many, and listened carefully to the radio shows that gave special attention to the American black artists who were being ignored elsewhere.

A weird new instrument called the 'electric bass' was invented around this time. *Melody Maker*, a weekly newspaper, emerged as one of the outstanding jazz periodicals of the era. The paper, however, dismissed the electrified instrument and called it a juiced-up silly toy, not to be used for anything but magnified amplification in dance bands. The electric bass, they warned, should be scorned by jazzmen of quality. Reg, though, liked the booming resonance and whiplash sounds generated by the wired-up guitar.

In March of 1955, when Reg had just celebrated his eighth birthday, Charlie 'Bird' Parker died, and something went out of the wild jazz fever that had possessed Britain since the war. There was little happening musically to take its place, and the Britains occupied themselves with the usual pap, the same tear-jerking vocalists they always relied on when nothing else was happening – Dickie Valentine or the sultry Lita Rosa. Reg went to see Dean Martin and Jerry Lewis films, and Rosemary was a family favorite.

Meanwhile, the newspapers kept reporting the wild rhythm and blues frenzy sweeping the U.S., afflicting its teenagers with an uncontrollable madness. Jazz-oriented *Melody Maker* condemned this new music and other such low-life songs as 'Shake, Rattle and Roll' as 'prostitution of the black man's blues.' But the British kids were getting interested.

'My mother introduced me to rock 'n' roll,' Reg was to credit her much later. 'One day she came home with "ABC Boogie," by Bill Haley, and when I heard it I nearly flipped out. My mother, she was always well up on what was going on.'

Reg's home life might not have always been pleasant during those years, though. His parents' relationship wasn't harmonious. Possibly to create a buffer between himself and the marital tensions he couldn't understand, the bewildered nine-year-old spent more and more time with his rock 'n' roll 45s and his piano experimentation. Quite sophisticated musically, he started taking formal piano lessons, lessons which at first seemed as if they were going nowhere. They were disastrous, in fact, because young Reggie didn't like traditional music at all.

The Dwights had hired the wrong teacher. Imagine the scene: little Reggie, his hair slicked down and parted on one side, perched on the bench. 'Well, my boy, have you practiced your middle C études sufficiently to play them for me today?' the wizened old instructor demanded. 'Ah, alas no. It seems you haven't. You must, I insist, have them mastered by next Thursday or I shan't be able to continue as your instructor. You will attend to the Bach and the Chopin, too, with special attention to the timing. And now, let's run through your assignment for today, Beethoven's Concerto in D Minor. Ready – a-one, a-two, a-three...'

'He was being forced to play classics when he wanted to play popular tunes,' Sheila Dwight recalled. 'It wasn't until he was eleven or twelve that I found him a new teacher who let him play pop tunes and from that time on, this was all he was interested in.'

Meanwhile, the rock 'n' roll plague was seeping into every English household. Older youths read the news and relayed it to the eager ears of Reg. They told him about Bill Haley's firebrand tour of the U.S. and how rock was the new rage. As a matter of fact, the king of the new rock music had played a concert in a southern U.S. city called Birmingham, located in the violent state of Alabama. The music was so tough and funky that the White Citizens' Council, a racist vigilante group, stormed in to break up the show, screaming that rock 'n' roll equalled 'sin, degradation and communism.' Their sentiments were echoed by moderate groups across the Western World. Even so, by 1957 Britishers' ears were glued and their bodies rocking to 'The Saints' Rock & Roll,' Bill Haley's adaptation of the Negro gospel song. Next, a single called 'Blackboard Jungle,' with the Comets' sound track 'Rock Around the Clock,' hit the United Kingdom. Suddenly all hell broke loose.

In Manchester, ten youths were fined for 'unusually insulting behavior' after leaving the *Jungle* film. On a Saturday night the rhythm-crazed youngsters held up traffic and trampled flower beds in Piccadilly Gardens after they stumbled out of the rocking theater. In Croydon, during performances fans stamped their feet, chanted, and shouted, 'We want rock 'n' roll.' Teen-age Britain was going rock crazy while the adults desperately tried to stem the tide.

Reggie Dwight was listening intently. The tunes might have rocked in his head day and night. He couldn't sleep. He was possessed with rock 'n' roll fever. The Top Twenty roared and rattled out of his King Brothers as he squeezed out the Platters' 'The Great Pretender,' Bill Haley's 'Hot Diggedity,' 'Tutti Frutti' by the amazing Little Richard, Bloodnock's 'Rock 'n' Roll Call,' and the heart-throbbing 'A Tear Fell,' by Teresa Brewer and Pat Boone's 'I'll Be Home.'

'Should We Surrender to the Teen-agers?' the *Melody Maker* headlines blasted. 'Should our teenagers be given the chance of hearing all the new Americans, even if our disc jockeys don't like them?'

'Yeah man,' squeaked myopic Reggie, now wearing glasses as he pounded out a Little Richard boogie on the King Brothers.

In America, Elvis Presley was being hailed as the 'Newest Teen-age Craze.' Doris Day starred in *Calamity Jane*, but Reggie liked *It's Magic*, the 1949 movie, better.

One fall, 'Hound Dog' entered the charts at No. 20, the next week it was 5, then 1. Then 'It's Only You' by the Platters took over. At the same time, Elvis's 'Heartbreak Hotel' broke like a sexy blue thunderstorm over England. Mrs. Dwight ran out and bought both 'Heartbreak Hotel' and 'Hound Dog.' Reggie zapped them on the phonograph.

> You ain nuthinbudder houn dogger
> A-crockin all time
> You achin rectinbubber houn dogger

> Crockin' all tine
> Where ailin' nudderhuder Rabidan
> You ain no frien of mine.

What did it all mean? It didn't matter; Reg loved it. On the music scene the press was howling. Croaked one jazz critic, 'Many times have I heard bad records, but for sheer repulsiveness coupled with . . . incoherence, "Hound Dog" hits a new low in my experience.'

'ROCK SETS IN' blasted a news headline as Jerry Lee Lewis was discovered as the new menace: 'Lewis is a downright disgrace,' the press spluttered. 'Attacking the Steinway like an enraged buffalo, he finished his act in a surge of saliva and sweat, hair hanging, his feet on the piano keys.' 'He's the greatest performer of them all,' the neighbor boy said to Reg, who knew it had to be true.

Reg was holding his breath until Jerry Lee's tour arrived in London. But in May, 1957, the staid London Hotel where Lee was booked asked the musician to leave. They were shocked, the hotel manager said, by Jerry's thirteen-year-old child bride (and his cousin, some say). The twenty-seven shows that Jerry Lee Lewis had scheduled were cancelled after silence greeted his first appearance. 'I sho' hope you all ain't half as dead as you sound,' said Jerry Lee to the disapproving audience. 'Go home, crumb, baby snatcher,' was the response. 'It's just jealousy,' said Jerry's young wife, Myra. But the bubble had burst, the ball of fire was out – except in the imagination of a boy like Reggie Dwight where it smoldered and flared up brighter and brighter with the passing days.

Reggie Dwight knew he could play the piano pretty well, but being a rock 'n' roll hero was just another fantasy he shared with every other kid. Reggie put the worn Jerry Lee Lewis disc on the record player; and when the smashing chords rolled out, with Jerry Lee screaming ,'I'm the killer,' Reg might have run to the mirror to watch himself going through the writhing wild motions of the piano master. Reggie, his fat little body shaking soundlessly and rolling with exertion, grimaced in silent mouthings of the line, 'I'm the killer.'

It was a delirious dream, Elton John remembered later, the pubescent kid, shy, overweight, flailing about to the rhythms of the rock 'n' roll madman from across the water. He might have thought, 'I wish this would happen to me; it's gotta happen to me.' Yet deep down he knew that in spite of his fat, his shyness, his nearsighted eyes, and the pressures to conform to middle-class ambitions, he knew that someday he would be a star. Not a singer, but *somebody*, like Ferrante and Teicher maybe – a pianist. 'I'll probably wind up putting out records like Bent Fabric,' he later admitted, 'sort of like an English version of the Ventures, only on the piano.'

Reggie played constantly. He had a natural ear and couldn't forget a melody if he tried. Tunes ran through his head all day, when he was trying to do his schoolwork or when he was out playing soccer with the neighborhood boys. 'I don't like the lessons, though,' he complained to a friend. 'And I don't like practising either.' But he played every pop tune he heard perfectly and without hesitation on the first try. His mother knew he was a genius.

CHAPTER 4

When Reg was ten, his father and mother divorced. The split was the result of a lingering unhappiness which was not without its effect on Reg. He was never to talk much about those years after the breakup. Who knows how much loneliness, anxiety – and unwarranted guilt – young Reggie stored up during that time? He was an only child, without even a brother or sister to share the tears of confusion with. His mother was still his best friend, though, and he hated to see her suffer.

Yet, during those sad years there were wonderful moments of fun and fantastic music floating in the air. Besides the buck shots of rock 'n' roll soaring over from the U.S., there was the marvelous popular fare called music hall that Reg could go to anytime.

English musical roots are very special and very narrow. British music hall, the kind that Reg and his friends and parents went to, was pure kitsch. The music hall started out as working-class people's entertainment. Originating in small pubs, it became so popular that the music-comedy clown and juggling acts had to be staged in giant halls where everybody could smoke foul-smelling cigars, gorge themselves with food, and swill down the grog while occasionally paying attention to the show. There were acrobats, contortionists, tightrope walkers and dizzying trapeze artists. There were comedians and song-and-dance routines. Everything was accompanied by plunkety-plunk piano and singing-strings orchestration. If the crowd liked the show, it cheered and took the performer to its heart. If it didn't, all the food in the audience landed in his face. It was a bawdy, rollicking world where friends met, fame was won, and everybody had a holiday.

It is only natural that when Reggie discovered American rock he would be attracted to the music hall's theatrical aspects which he knew so well. Even if at the time, he couldn't rock with the same natural ease and assurance as his American cousins, he could absorb the theatrical genius of the music hall and store it up for later.

Later, such groups as Elton John's, the Stones, David Bowie, the Moody Blues, Emerson, Lake and Palmer, Jethro Tull, and Genesis would dive into theatrical pretension with more real fire and knowhow than any American because of their exposure to the music hall. The closest Americans ever came to music-hall rock was the Alice Cooper show. Elton John learned the secret of performing before a difficult audience from the greatest stars of the music hall, and it still shows in his stage presence and showmanship.

At the music halls, while others were stuffing candy and food into their mouths, the adolescent Reg, still as rolypoly as ever, was trying to diet. He was enrolled at Harrow High School – and the other kids had been making fun of his weight.

School turned out to be a less than happy experience for Reg, and every day became an exercise in decision-making: Was he going to force himself to enter the gloomy gray halls of the all-boy institution, or was he going to skip classes? Was he going to hop a train for Piccadilly Circus, or carefully complete his homework sheets? Was he going to hang out at the record shop, while away the day at the piano, or listen to a lecture on geography?

The decision was inevitable. He wanted to perform. 'In those days you weren't allowed to perform in public until you were thirteen years old,' Sheila later confided. 'Otherwise he'd have been a child prodigy. He would have definitely won the talent contests that were going on at that time.'

As it was, Reg won a part-time music scholarship to the venerable old institution, the Royal Academy of Music, in London.

'I could have gone to the Academy full time,' Elton later admitted ruefully, 'if I'd worked harder.' But even going to the Academy part-time was no picnic. Even though it brought him in contact with all forms of music, Elton looks back painfully on the hours of étude practice and theory classes he endured in the windowless studios of the strict old school. He and ninety-odd other students, hand-picked from the British Isles, sweated to meet the Academy's severe standards of musical excellence. The budding concert pianists were urged to devote their entire young lives to the mastery of the fine points of Bach, Beethoven, Debussy, Chopin, Rachmaninoff as well as to the techniques of harpsichord, organ, and stringed instruments. 'But I don't like classical music,' Reggie would protest to the venerable maestro. 'I want to be a rock 'n' roll singer and play in a band,' he pleaded.

'It was the same in school,' he adds now. 'I was probably a good enough scholar to go to a university, but I never tried more than thirty percent. I was always into pop music or football and I just squeezed through my exams. I was very lazy.'

On Saturday mornings, when he was scheduled for his private lesson at the Royal Academy, Reggie picked up his sheet music, grabbed a hot crumpet off the stove, and jumped on the train to London. Reaching the center of the capital, he transferred to the Circle line. By the time the tube screeched into the stop for the Academy, the reluctance which had been welling up in Reg totally possessed his body. He was almost paralyzed. He sat motionless in his seat as the people filed out of the train, the doors slid closed, and it took off again with a slight lurch. All the morning, round and round, under the city of London, Reg sat on the moving train. All afternoon, countlessly circling the city in the darkness of the subway tunnels, the young man sat staring out of the window into nothing. It happened more Saturdays than he cared to admit.

'So far as education went,' he explained later, 'and learning the piano, I never achieved what I could have done. But that was because I knew I wanted to do something else. I wanted to sing like Elvis.

'At school all I wanted to do was get into the glitter world of show biz, I knew that as long as I had something to do with the music business – then I'd be happy. I was records mad. I loved singing and playing, too, of course. I even earned a few quid playing in pubs.'

Every Friday night after the dinner hour, the local pubs filled to the brim. All the neighboring villagers, young and old, would step out to these centers of social activity for a bit of live entertainment and a shot of spirits. Waiters scurried to and fro with half a dozen mugs of foaming ale in each hand. The sound of laughter rose higher, muffling the noise of the buskers warming up their folksy instruments to play. Reggie, sitting in a booth with his chums, suddenly asked himself, Why wasn't he up there performing? He could play folk, as well as the old fave pop tunes. He could even play skiffle.

Reggie, like many other British musicians, was going through a skiffle stage. Skiffle, a loose combination of rhythm and blues and country music, was all the rage in the late fifties. It was very easy to play with homemade instruments like combs, washtubs, and chest basses. Its cheery good-timey quality made it perfect for the espresso coffee shops in London and the local pub scene. Reggie's favorite skiffle artist was Lonnie Donnegan, who achieved international fame with his 'Did Your Chewing Gum Lose Its Flavor on the Bedpost Overnight?'

Looking over the local talent, Reggie decided there was no reason why he shouldn't be up on the stage performing. He could pound the ivories better than most of them anyway. What difference if he was only thirteen?

He decided to go out and do something about it. Scouting the Harrow area, Reg discovered that a nearby inn in Northwood needed a piano player. Northwood Inn featured boring English food – beef and kidney pie on Thursdays – plus a boring middle-class clientele every day of the week. But it was a job, and it paid well. Every Friday, Saturday, and Sunday night Reg tramped up the hills to tinkle the keys for the rowdy customers.

'I used to take my box around,' he recalled to a British journalist, 'and people would put donations in it. I was making a fortune compared to the rest of the kids. I was geting about thirty-five quid a week, I think.'

It was the beginning of Reg Dwight's life-long love

affair with the goddess of Riches and Wealth. Within a year he had raked in enough quid to buy an electric piano and amplifiers. He had a flair for making money that would occasionally ebb, but would always surge back even stronger in the ten years to come.

Reg was seldom at home, unless he was practising. When he wasn't playing in the clubs, he was going to those 'package shows' which the British kids flocked to in the early sixties. 'I saw Roy Orbison, Del Shannon and Neil Sedaka, Gary U.S. Bonds, Frankie Valle, and the Four Seasons [whom he was later to bring back to life on such cuts as 'Benny and the Jets.']. Even today I sound like Frankie Valle and the Four Seasons,' Elton John claimed years later. Bobby Darin sailed into Great Britain to play to sold-out houses across the Empire. 'I find British audiences to be the noisiest in the world,' he commented. As rock 'n' roll's second wave broke and slid up the British beaches, the old Bluesmen, Muddy Waters, B. B. King, and Hank Williams began to fill the airwaves too. Paul Anka, Billy Fury, rocked on while Chubby Checker broke entirely new ground with 'The Twist' in 1960. Reg was thirteen going on fourteen when Elvis's 'It's Now or Never' was No. 1, followed by Orbison's 'Only the Lonely.' But the memorable Ray Charles, Brenda Lee, the Drifters, Johnny Tillitson, and Brook Benton washed over the United Kingdom with the muted tones of a soft crooning jive that lulled the Britishers into a temporary calm. It was no wonder that the name of Elton John's first group would be called Bluesology.

The early sixties were an incredibly seminal period for British rock 'n' roll groups. Kids, barely out of their knickers, formed skiffle, folk, and even Haley-based rock bands and played for every event they could possibly use for an excuse. Rock music was more than a hobby or after-school sport; it was a total obsession. The youths, when they weren't playing, listened intently to the music with perhaps even more pure concentration than their American counterparts and tried to recreate it in their own bands. Their bands formed, broke up, and reformed with such fluidity that often even the members themselves didn't know who was in whose group. Such freedom of movement and adaptability marked the style of British rock for years to come. And Reg Dwight's band, Bluesology, was born in this rich, chaotic ground.

Bluesology got its start when Reg was fourteen, and he and some buddies from Harrow met nightly to jam. A warm and energetic young schoolmate named Mick Inkpen banded away on a crude set of skins which hardly qualified to be called drums. Another adolescent named Stuart Brown played a snappy guitar, but it was scarcely a mature sound, more like the whining and twanging of a building crane on wheels trying to climb up a steep hill. Finally, another chubby lad, Rex Bishop, laid down some thudding bass beats, which, although they weren't smooth, contained enough hot raw power to charge up the crowds in those sweaty neighborhood bars. Bluesology would play; and here in the youth clubs, milk bars, scout huts, as well as in the dark century-old pub rooms with the foaming pints of Watney's Red Barrel passing over the low, heavy-beamed bar, Elton began to mature as a performer.

Elton's adolescent band had just one ten-watt amplifier with the piano left acoustic. The first tunes they played were so unforgettable no one could remember them from one gig to the next. But gradually the young band got into playing Jimmy Witherspoon numbers. Nevertheless, Bluesology was always playing the wrong stuff in those days. They were about two months too late, or three years too early, never playing the right thing at the right time but always appealing to minority tastes. Tuning up the honky-tonk piano, Reggie would look out into the restless crowds milling about the pub and glance at the ancient sad-eyed Newfoundland retriever that always stood guard inside. He sensed the rising surge of excitement as the crowd began to anticipate the gig to come.

Bluesology was picking up a reputation in the outlying districts of London. People began to arrive at horrible little joints just to hear the jumpy ragtime riffs and mellow blue notes Reggie Dwight squeezed out of his rickety old upright. The young quartet toured the club-and-pub scene around London for almost two years, lurching and stumbling at first, but building up steam and somehow managing to delight their audiences.

The year Reggie turned sixteen, he had a grave decision to make. According to the British system, he had to decide if he was going to pursue his education and choose a university, or go off into the world with only the minimum of formal education. But Reggie knew his destiny, and successful or not, he had to follow his heart and rock 'n' roll.

As soon as he finished his A-levels, Reg Dwight decided to put an end to his formal education. And Bluesology, his weekend band, became a full-time, serious venture for him.

Nineteen sixty-three was a historical year. And the seeds of the Elton Show were sown in those days. 'Those were very shaky, exhausting times,' Elton John recalled, as he later looked back on Bluesology's apprenticeship period.

The sky was always black, the fog as thick as the proverbial soup when the Bluesology band members prepared to set out for a gig in an outlying part of the country. They all met at a predesignated place. Picking up their guitars, amps, battered and scarred from many such rude morning jolts, the hardy fellows heaved some of the equipment upon the back of their Ford and shoved the bulk into the rear compartment. Reg, however, gently lifted his electric piano from its stand and eased himself into the passenger seat in front, all the time holding the delicate instrument against his body. The car nosed off down the street and into the faintly glowing pink horizon.

'Those gigs were really unbelievable,' Elton remembered. 'We had no manager to hump our gear around then. For instance, I did a gig in London at 4:30 P.M., went up to Birmingham and done a 'double' and come back home and play the Cue Club at 4:30 in the morning. I'll never know how I managed to lift my gear over those six hundred sweaty people.' 'Unbelievable. . . .' 'It was good grounding,' Elton admitted to *New Musical Express*. 'That's the way and where you learn. When you look back on it, you're glad you did it. I've paid my dues, and I never want to do it again.' Bluesology logged months of hard work.

Paying dues was a process that distinguishes thoroughbred performers from pretenders. Reggie Dwight, as he was transformed into Elton John, indeed served his time. While Bluesology and Elton John were logging hours in sweaty dives, Reggie Dwight worked as a tea boy at Mills Music Company.

The American equivalent of a tea boy is a 'gofer'. The term began in Hollywood, where young lads dying for a chance to work in movies hung around sets and ran errands. Producers and directors would order, 'Go for coffee,' 'Go for more cold beer.' Eventually the errand boy became known as the gofer. In England they were called tea boys because they not only served the tea, but boiled the water for the instant artificial energy. The tea boy, Reg Dwight, boiled tea in the studios, in the executives' offices, and on the main halls.

While he was running his legs off for the employees of Mills Music, Reg was also raking in quid doing session work on cheap records. He did one reputable back-up vocal on Stevie Wonder's single 'Signed, Sealed and Delivered'. Reggie did all the 'oooohs', and 'aahhhhhs', while Dave Byron (later to become lead singer for Uriah Heep) did all the leads.

Then he did a cover for a Dutch record company of 'Saved by the Bell', by the Bee Gees. He went around for weeks singing his Robin Gibb imitation.

But Reg's major interest was still Bluesology. One Saturday morning the band and he motored up to Kilburn for an audition at the State cinema, where there was going to be a contest between bands. There were thousands of groups milling about, each one of them staking everything on the possibility of winning the prize for best amateur talent. Each band had to play two or three numbers, and Bluesology was nervous, but managed to carry off their songs without a major flaw or upheaval.

Afterward the air was fraught with tension as the groups stood around waiting for the judge's final verdict. The boys in Reggie's band were leaning against a wall, trying to look nonchalant when a man approached them.

'Hello, chaps,' he said. Reggie mumbled a reply. 'I'm from the Roy Tempest agency,' the man said with a friendly smile. 'Perhaps you fellows would be interested in turning professional.'

It was a stunning surprise. An agent and some guaranteed work. The Bluesology boys were, for once, speechless. 'Well, ah, I'll, ah, have to ask me mother,' Reggie might have mumbled awkwardly.

It was no problem getting Mrs. Dwight's permission. Any concern she initially had over Reggie's career was dispelled after going to a few gigs with him. Sometimes Reg and the boys in Bluesology took her to see Georgie Fame or Cliff Bennett. As a matter of fact, Sheila Dwight's favorite band was an organ-soul group called the Paramounts, who would later evolve into Procol Harum.

Bluesology and Mrs. Dwight gave a rousing, 'Yes, indeed,' to the agent from Roy Tempest. A few weeks later they found themselves as the back-up group for Wilson Pickett. Soon, however, Pickett's guitarist decided he didn't like the young Bluesers' sound. Next came a few solos with soul artist Major Lance. After Major Lance, they played with a quick succession of people: Patti LaBelle twice, the original Drifters for two gigs, a whole tour with Doris Troy, and a whole tour with the Ink Spots and Billy Stewart. On off months Bluesology made the traditional pilgrimage of British bands. The Beatles had done it in the 1950s, and now Bluesology went to Hamburg for several months. The first trip outside the island empire expanded Reggie's horizons. As he walked the streets of the German port town, he explored the famous red-light district where the prostitutes sat in red-velvet windows and turned their bodies into fantasy objects. On the way home from Germany, Bluesology whipped through Sweden and then down through the south of France for a month, luxuriating in the sun at Saint Tropez.

With all the new-found excitement in being a professional band, it was in some ways still a miserable existence. Bluesology was a chaotic group. There was no clear-cut leader and none with real business experience. They still staggered through the weeks, not ever knowing for sure what was coming up next. Bluesology was making the grade, though. No longer did they have to play dives like the Scotch of Saint James, but could switch to the marquee-artist circuit, a round of clubs which included the Cromwellian, the World's End, the Bag O' Nails, and many other English name night spots. But instant success was by no means waiting in the wings.

A year passed, with aimless gigs flying by. John Kennedy was shot in the U.S. and the reverberations of the stateside turmoil rocked the rest of the world. The Beatles, who had already been the hottest band in England for two years suddenly took hold in the colonies, and it seemed as if British rock 'n' roll was the answer to all America's problems. The rock world was booming on the east side of the Atlantic. Rock groups mushroomed overnight, stars were made every fifteen minutes, and teenagers turned into millionaires as gold records stacked up like pancakes. One night Reg met a gravelly-voiced rooster with whom he would be friends for a decade to come. The meeting took place at the Conservative Club in Kenton when Reggie was only seventeen.

'I remember the first time I saw Rod Stewart,' he said. 'I was still in school then, and I asked him for his autograph. I just went up to the front of the pub where he was singing and said, "Excuse me, Mr. Stewart, can I have your autograph?" It was wild. He used to come up on stage with a scarf around his neck and sing, "Good Morning Little School Girl". I thought he was great.' The bantam-sized rocker was hanging out with a long, tall gent who was about to play a crucial role in the next scene of Reginald Dwight's dramatic rise to stardom.

CHAPTER 5

Every night, men from all over greater London would flock to the Cromwellian club, famous for the rousing games of poker which went on full steam every night. There were also gaming tables set up for chemin de fer, craps, and other games of chance. On crisp autumn nights in 1966 a long tall man would stride into the club and pull up a chair to whichever of the games would provide the highest stakes and the sweetest thrills.

On one particular night, however, the gambler was bored with cards and the persistent run of sixes on the dice so he said, 'I'm shoving off, mates, gonna head downstairs to the disco, see ya later.'

The tall man was the legendary Long John Baldry. Baldry's decision to descend to the cavelike cell where Reg's little band played was another historic moment in the life of the stubby keyboard man.

Baldry, a six-foot seven-inch hunk of massive British bluesman, his arms like crane joints with hooks on the ends, had already won fame for his interpretation of Negro R&B. On that night he was twenty-five years old and had already been playing the English blues circuits for nine years, his reputation for wild antics and ribald stories keeping pace with his fabled guitar and raucous blues vocals.

That night he listened to the Bluesology gig and after the last set he called the group over to his table. It was late and before long people started joining the conversation, attracted by the presence of Baldry, who ranked along with

John Mayall and Alexis Korner as a fountainhead of British R&B. As usual Long John began to rap about how he got started; Baldry's story was classic rhythm and blues. Reg might have listened intently as Baldry recounted the roots of the Rolling Stones and his role in their growth. Then suddenly he broke off in midsentence and stared right at Reggie. 'What are you planning to do with this Bluesology group?' he might have asked. 'Do you want to join me as my back-up?' Reg was floored. He had seen Baldry in action and had dreamed of being part of the world in which Long John moved. Reg Dwight was nineteen and raring to take the next step to fame.

New Year's 1967 arrived. It was the year that was destined to bring to full blossom all the optimism of the young, vibrant counter culture, sometimes known as the 'hippie movement', sometimes called the 'flower generation'. It was a time which ran on the fuel of rock 'n' roll as a kind of psychic nuclear energy, fusion, and fission. Music was in the air everywhere.

In 1967 John Baldry took over the reins of Bluesology and whipped up the amateurish five-man band into a piping hot nine-piece touring group whose name quickly spread throughout the club circuits in England. At first Baldry considered the boys merely a back-up group for his artists, but soon they were gaining near-equal status. By August they were playing spots like the Bluesville '67 clubs in Brentwood and Ipswich, billed in all the major newspapers and club listings as the John Baldry Show.

This was Reg's first really big break. He was now going to see some real pro action as a part of a famous group, a band whose sound was going to make the big time and even land a record-label contract. The only small but persistent worry he had was that he wasn't allowed to sing in or write the tunes for any of the songs in the sets. There was no place for the voice of Reginald Dwight in the John Baldry Show.

As the band began to be transformed under the knowing hands of the older rocker, however, Reg could feel the currents of success swirling and mounting around him.

By now Bluesology had added to its lineup a sax blower named Elton Dean, a cornet player named Mark Charig, and Neil Hubbard (later to go on to Grease Band fame). Also contributing a brilliant guitar was handsome Caleb Quaye, a black American who would play an important role in the bringing to life of Elton John. Also in the Baldry line-up was Pete Gavin (later to go on to the group Head, Hands and Feet).

The John Baldry Show was a traveling zoo. With wildman Baldry in charge of setting up dates and overseeing all the organizational matters, the musical caravan careened from one engagement to another. They played anywhere, anytime, running from one end of the Empire to the other.

It was during these years that Reg met the best musicians England had to offer. In addition, he got the chance to jam with many of the biggest visiting rock and soul musicians from the mythical land of America. Yet the actual day-to-day life of Baldry's touring blues band was the most gruelling existence imaginable.

No music companies were drooling over them either, and even under Baldry's direction Bluesology hadn't really gotten off the ground. It was by no means the internationally acclaimed group they thought it should be, so Long John decided the only way to gain attention was to make a commercial record. The band promptly cut a track called 'Let the Heartaches Begin'. And the single immediately, amazingly, soared up the British charts eleven places in one week. 'It couldn't have happened at a better time,' chortled Baldry. 'I was planning to assault the cabaret field.'

And assault they did. It was a step up the booking ladder, Reg supposed, playing in the more expensive, orchestrated supper spots. But it nearly drove the bouncy piano pumper crazy. Bluesology was sacrificing its considerable lineup of talent for instant hit-making potboilers.

'John shouldn't be doing it this way,' Reg reportedly told a friend. ' "Heartaches" is the wrong song. It's affecting him personally, and I think he's beginning to realize it. He should be respected, be in the same position that John Mayall and Alexis Korner are in. He should have everyone's respect because he's found so many people.'

Instead of respect, Baldry's band had bookings in every club and cabaret north of Birmingham. It was a dreadful part of the country up there, where the sun seldom shone and the furze- and moss-covered hills stretched bleakly as far as the eye could see. It was as gloomy as earth's last outpost.

Bluesology was the most popular jumping band in those parts, and whenever there were no other gigs to be had, they always knew they could turn their sights north, pack their gear, and head up to that frontier for a month to make enough quid to tide themselves over.

One night, right in the middle of a dance-hall gig, even as he was pumping out the bouncy tune, Reg had a sudden chilling moment of doubt. He played 'Let the Heartaches Begin' automatically; but inside his mind was racing madly.

He hated this northern-club scene. It was really depressing. He didn't want to join another band, though, where he'd just be the organist, shoved to the rear of the stage. What could he do? He had been on the road for four years. 'Maybe I've made the wrong decision, after all,' he might have thought with horror. 'Maybe I should have gone to school, found a reputable career, should have gone into business as all the other chaps from Harrow did. Or concentrated on classical piano – I could have become a piano teacher or a musical director in a public-school choir. I just can't go on playing "Let the Heartaches Begin" every night.'

In Bluesology there were three or four really huge egos. 'I know what it's like to be in a band with strong personalities,' Reg Elton John was later to tell an aspiring teenage piano player. 'There were some people who thought they should be monster stars. And that climate is unhealthy.'

Reg Elton John Dwight was already working out some beginning strategy for his own touring band, a band he had not consciously dreamed a fat, shy, insecure young man like himself could ever have. He would never have believed that cold midnight in the Northlands that only three years later he would be telling a reporter from a national news weekly that, 'There's only one ego in my band, and that's me.'

The husky-throated piano man was to learn from the dramatic moments with the other members of Bluesology that it could not be 'Elton John and his back-up band', by any means. 'No, I wouldn't want it to be like that,' he added quickly. 'Everyone would chip in their own ideas. I would never say you must do this and play that. But everyone would know, for example, that if I say we don't do a certain song one night, then that's it. There would never be any question.'

In Bluesology, though, Reg had no voice, especially on stage.

CHAPTER 6

'There are so many good people going around in bands who are afraid to take the plunge or don't get the chance. They really want to break out, but they daren't,' Elton John confided three years later. 'The only reason I did was because I was so depressed and miserable. I just had to.' One morning while on tour with Baldry in Newcastle, Reg picked up a copy of the *New Musical Express*, the English rock weekly, and caught sight of an advertisement placed by Liberty UA Records saying:

> Liberty leaving EMI, going independent, needs singers and talent.

Liberty Records was clamoring for song writers, and they were holding open auditions for any hopeful. Reg didn't know which way to turn. He knew he wanted to come off the road. 'I'm literally becoming a touring vegetable,' he thought, squeezing his arm and feeling nothing at all.

So he made an appointment with Liberty, and a few days later, he eagerly ran to the famous Regent Sound Studios where the auditions were being held. By the time he walked into the acoustically tiled recording studio with its deep, sound-muffling carpets and vacant walls, he was trembling like a bowl of jelly. So nervous he was, he could barely pull a sound through his lips. He presented himself to the man in charge, Ray Williams. 'I, ah, um, I can't write lyrics and I really can't sing well because I wasn't singing with Bluesology, you see.'

The engineer behind the taping panel replied gently, 'Just sing five songs, if you please.'

'God,' he might have replied to himself, 'I don't know five songs.' Nevertheless, he treated them to a couple of tunes he had prepared. 'I haven't sung for years,' he might have thought. 'What am I doing here?' But plowing through his rapidly numbing musical memory, he finally came up with some old schmaltzy numbers and treated them to a forgettable performance of Jim Reeves's 'He'll Have to Go,' and 'I Love you Because.'

The Liberty representatives listened quietly, but even before Reg ended the last chords, he knew the sad results. 'Sorry, no chance here,' they delivered the verdict.

'You can't blame them,' Reg might have thought as he readied himself for a quick exit. 'I was pretty terrible.'

But within the darkened rooms of the Regent recording studio, lit at various times by one rock god or another, two very young men were destined to find each other – one, the blond, boyish melodist, and the other, the shy country lyricist, Bernie Taupin.

As Reg was fleeing the studio, he was stopped by producer Ray Williams, who suggested he take a look at some lyric sheets Liberty had received from a fellow in Lincolnshire, another reject talent Liberty didn't want.

'OK, I'll take a look at them,' Reg probably mumbled, his face still burning from the embarrassment in the tryout room. The words on the page already had begun to spark off little notes and melody phrases in his head. 'They sure are better and more poetic than anything I've been able to write,' he might have thought. Reg himself could not string two lines together, as Liberty Records had detected, much less a verse and chorus. But when he read over the poems of Bernie Taupin he felt a strange, eerie flow of inspiration. He decided he must try to contact the poet. Ironically, at this time Bernie had also answered an ad placed in the *New Musical Express* by a composer looking for a lyricist. Reg Dwight had not placed that ad, but he *was* the right composer for Bernie, and immediately, uncannily, as if it had been preordained, he knew that Bernie Taupin was going to be very important to him. It was the weirdest chance encounter in a million lifetimes, although it wasn't really an encounter because Reg didn't actually meet the lad from Lincolnshire until Bernie had written the words to over twenty songs for him. 'The first twenty songs we wrote without seeing each other, and crude things they were, although they got published by the Hollies' company,' Reg explained later. 'We just started writing songs to supplement our salaries and my Bluesology wages. And I did odd demos and session gigs with all sorts of people.' Reg and Bernie had yet to meet face to face.

The pace of life suddenly began to quicken. Reg was composing freely, he was gigging with Bluesology, and he was playing and singing back-up with everybody imaginable. He did the original demo for the Brotherhood of Man's 'United We Stand.' He didn't like to admit it, but he also sang on the Avenue records, the same kind of ear-wash canned tunes played in supermarkets on both sides of the Atlantic. 'I had a ball,' Reg confessed. 'We'd have a right laugh on those sessions doing Andy Fairweather-Low and the whole lot.' As a plus, his voice was improving daily with this practice.

In the meantime, Reg was getting daily packets of mail

from Lincolnshire. Taupin religiously sent sheets of lyric paper overflowing with fragile images, other-worldly visions and passion. Out of the verses Reg worked out melodies, rhythmic patterns, and architectural palaces of sound. Taupin's words had unleashed a creative demon in Elton. Now all he needed was a studio in which to sound out the new melodies which were literally tumbling out of him.

One day a mate at Liberty Records dropped a useful bit of information. An enormous company called Dick James Music was becoming very liberal with their sound studio. It was Dick James's idea to let artists come in and record what they wanted. His artists usually had a tremendous amount of freedom as far as recording and producing was concerned, and it was rumored that anyone could wander in and mess around with the primitive but efficient two-track console.

Reg hustled over to Dick James's establishment, a musical landmark located around the corner from a kosher delicatessen near the tin pan alley equivalent in London, and began to record his songs during his spare time.

Dick James occupied a special kind of place in the hearts of British rockers. James himself was a short, pudgy fellow who started his musical career singing the voice of Robin Hood for the internationally videoed series about the forest swashbuckler. Tuning in the telly each week for the exciting Sherwood adventures, Robin Hood fans would be greeted to the deep bass voice of Dick James booming out through the speakers as Robin and Little John galloped along the road: 'Robin Hood, Robin Hood, riding through the glen. Robin Hood, Robin Hood, with his band of men . . .' It was a famous lyric, but few people knew the merry chap behind it. Soon, however, Dick James was making noise for himself. He moved into the music-publishing field.

'His success came overnight,' confided a young, well-dressed employee of Dick James Music. 'Dick had a very good friend who called him up one day, and said, "I've got a group who've got a very good song, you might be interested in publishing it." Dick came over. The song happened to be "I Want to Hold Your Hand," and the group was the Beatles. Dick signed them up, and, as they say, the rest is history.

'Dick did not, however, discover Elton John,' continued the elegant young A&R man, 'although he would probably say he did.'

While he was tinkering around in the studio, Reg was still moonlighting with Bluesology, and still miserable. He knew now that he had to start writing his own music and playing in his own band.

One day during a recording session at Dick James's studios, Reg noticed a tiny, dark-haired fellow blending into the shadows in the corner. 'Who are you?' Reg asked as he approached him.

'Bernie Taupin,' was the quiet reply from the man with the large eyes and smooth, almost perfect face.

'Oh, it's you,' Reg might have said, taken aback. Then followed five minutes of intense awkwardness as the two men, who'd worked together long-distance, stared at each other. Their eyes locked. Then the songwriter and the lyricist went off around the corner to have coffee and talk about the songs they had written together by proxy.

Bernie Taupin could have been dropped on earth from another planet, invented by a galactic mastermind to complete Reg Dwight's metamorphosis from a struggling chubbette on the keyboards into a soaring superstar whose melodious outpourings would razzle two continents.

Taupin was born in Rasen, Lincolnshire, the camping grounds of the real Robin Hood. At an early age, the young boy began plundering the rich images of the countryside to make poetry. On leaving school the mysterious, dreamy teenager wandered about the Midlands, the western lands of King Arthur and the Cotswolds, the lovely rolling hills of Shakespeare's birthplace. The poet Taupin took various odd jobs, laboring on local farms and working in factories during the cold months when the fields lay fallow. He constantly wrote poetic lines that usually fell on unreceptive ears.

Bernie was a gypsy with one earring, long hair, and bright tattered clothes. He dreamed and lived science fiction, *Winnie the Pooh* (he was later to name his Lincolnshire cottage 'Piglet in the Wilds'), American Wild West lore and heroic deeds executed by mythological figures.

When he met Reg Dwight, Taupin's prospects for becoming a recognized poet were virtually nil. Yet, even before Dick James discovered that the two were working at his studios overtime, they had written and recorded hundreds of tunes. The publisher, however, heard through the grapevine that the duo was using his facilities to make endless demos, and he decided to throw a purge. 'Who is this Reg Dwight,' he demanded, 'spending all my money in the studio?' Caleb Quaye, Reg's buddy from Mills Music and Bluesology was working as an engineer at DJM. When he heard about the ouster, he ran up to the headman's office and said to the Beatle-made mogul, 'Listen, let Reg go ahead, his work is outa sight.'

'Caleb saved our bacon,' Elton sighed later. 'Because James then signed us up for a ten-pound retainer. It was then that I could quit Baldry. The quid was enough to live on.'

The last gig Reg Dwight did with Baldry was on a Scottish tour. After the closing set, he flew back to London with Caleb, impatient to get back to his composing. But as they were clipping the Scottish clouds high above the highlands, the piano thumper turned to Quaye.

'You know,' he might have blurted out, 'I'm fed up with Reg Dwight.' 'What are you talking about?' the guitarist might have wondered, puzzling over the self-destructive ideas running through Reg's mind.

Reg decided he had to change his name. 'I can't be Reg Dwight if I'm going to be a singer,' he might have mused. 'I've got a record coming out, and it can't have Reg Dwight plastered all over it. Reg Dwight sounds like a cement mixer.'

As they flew toward London, Reg and his friend tossed around a number of names, but none of them was printable.

Suddenly Reg thought of the Bluesology gang with whom he'd spent the most exciting times of his life. Then it struck him like a flash – Elton Dean, the name of the snazzy sax man who was planning to leave Baldry to join the Soft Machine's progressive lineup. But no, he couldn't pinch Elton Dean's name.

What was a short name that sounded good with Elton? He had to make up his mind quickly before they landed in London.

Then Reg decided. Glancing around the plane, his eyes lit on the giraffelike bulk of Mr. John Baldry.

'Oh, Elton *John*, there you go,' he might have shouted.

Nobody actually liked it, Elton was later to admit. 'But it was the only one we could think of. Poor old Elton Dean's gone on to greater things as well since I pinched his name.'

'It's a name, at least, not a noise,' commented one friend.

Was it exciting to have a new name? 'Not really,' Elton explained later. 'Reg Dwight is exactly the same as Elton John.' Changing his name did him a lot of good, though, Elton admitted later to *Melody Maker*. 'I had a terrible inferiority complex, and to change my name helped me get away from it. At one point I wanted to change it again, but no one could come up with anything better.' The name just seemed to stick – another gift dropped from heaven along with Bernie Taupin.

'But I still can't get used to it,' Elton explained. 'Even now when people call me "Elton," I think they're putting me on, sending me up being very flash. But few people call me "Reg" anymore – even Dick started calling me Elton, which is very strange.'

Bernie and Elton eagerly signed a contract with Dick James. But the naïve duo wasn't at all familiar with James's style at the time and didn't realize that he wanted them to write Top Forty stuff, the Englebert Humperdinck sugar cubes that were floating in the pop air at that time. And the pair's first attempts to crank out commercial material proved fruitless. They recorded an entire album that James nixed. 'I was knocked out by that album at the time,' Elton admitted later. 'But I heard it last night and I was embarrassed.'

Struggling to write till-ringing ditties, Elton and Bernie's efforts were in vain. 'It's just getting too frustrating,' complained Elton, who thought he'd left frustration behind with Reg Dwight and Bluesology.

Dick James began to get peeved because the John-Taupin songs were not saleable. 'We were getting more and more down in the dumps because we thought we were writing what he wanted. He actually entered one of our songs in the Eurovision contest,' Elton later raved, 'and the song got into the last six places.'

There was incredible pressure on them to produce. They had indeed gotten into big business and were about to flounder in the heavy waters while desperately afraid of losing the headway they'd made. They wrote fast and furiously, as quickly as they could get the notes and words out. Then Elton and Bernie decided to take the advice of a famous hit-writing duo, Roger Cook and Roger Greenaway, who were able to give them some pointers to lift them out of their doldrums.

Although the Cook and Greenaway team wrote by means of a prearranged pattern derived from a Top Forty format, they quickly discouraged the younger team from doing so. The only reason the Cook-Greenaway team designed their songs to a formula was because it suited them best. The older partners were able to see immediately that the formula pattern was failing miserably with Bernie and Elton, and they quickly admonished the piano player, advising him and the Lincolnshire lad to write according to their own personal inspirations.

While Cook and Greenaway were advising them to write for themselves, the inexperienced twosome received a timely hint from Steve Brown, A&R man with Dick James Music. Steve, stopping by the studio where Elton was cutting a track, covered his ears and grimaced when he heard the bubbly sound coming from the studio speakers. 'This isn't very good,' he said bluntly. 'Why don't you write what you want to write?' Elton and Bernie had heard that bit of wisdom before, but when they got it straight from another Dick James employee, they realized it took an act of courage and faith. And they were desperate for some help and guidance at that point.

The partners were experiencing amazing disappointments. They were told to record countless songs they had penned in shameless imitation of the current favorites. And after they did manage to work them out, the songs would never be released.

Elton actually did manage to release one album on the Phillips label. It was called *I've Been Loving You* – and it was atrocious. He actually made a couple of singles on the Bluesology moniker, too, 'Come Back Baby' and 'Mr. Frantic.' The more left unsaid about both, the better.

Elton and Bernie churned out another single on Polydor, written and produced by Kenny Lynch, called 'Since I Met You, Baby,' which also went straight to the bottom and was buried. And after that, Elton cut 'I've Been Loving You,' one of his first as Elton John. It was a simpering Englebert Humperdinck-type effort. But very few people ever realized that Elton had such a history of cheap productions. Most people thought that the tasteful 'Lady Samantha' was his first song.

Steve Brown was responsible for 'Lady Samantha,' as he was for pushing Elton into the big time. Steve encouraged Elton every step of the way in his battles with Dick James, who was still insisting that the piano man pump out the Top Forty tunes. Steve, meanwhile, was gradually working his way into Elton's confidence, helping him to build up resistance against the businessman's pressure. And Steve finally won him over; Elton took Brown's advice and wrote 'Lady Samantha,' the product of his own imagination.

Steve Brown produced 'Lady Samantha,' a single, which despite 120 air plays on Radio One sold only about ten thousand copies. Yet at the same time, scores of discerning DJs like Tony Blackburn and Dave Symonds were raving about the record. It was played right across the board, and because of it Elton was asked to do a few live performances.

When Steve heard the blond keyboardsman at his piano he knew a phenomenal artist was in the making, and he asked Dick James if he could produce all the Elton John numbers. He got the nod from James at last, and the trio went into the studio to lay down some tracks.

Elton and Bernie were rapidly gaining confidence. On the heels of 'Lady Samantha' they recorded and released a new single 'Skyline Pigeon' with Cook-away Music Company. The romantic harpsichord rock-hymn with its vague lyrics full of wistful yearning got immediate air play. Critics stopped to listen to the vocalist. They were hearing a strong new voice playing a unique new arrangement. 'Skyline Pigeon' began to boil slowly. But there were still many other hurdles to be jumped before Elton John would become a major force in music.

CHAPTER 7

Nineteen sixty-nine was a strange year for rock 'n' roll in Great Britain. Woodstock had capped the main surge of the psychedelic power music in the U.S., but Britain's semi-equivalent, the Isle of Wight, was only looming on the horizon in January when the weirdo Bonzo Dog Doo Dah band (featuring Legs Larry Smith) released their smash single, 'I Am the Space Man.' Cream gave their farewell concert televised to the world on BBC from the Royal Albert Hall (of *Sgt. Pepper* fame). Jimi Hendrix injured a leg ligament in a fall on a stairway in New York and was voted 'Best Artist of the Year' by *Billboard* magazine. Soul provided the hottest new sounds around with Marvin Gaye's 'I Heard It Through the Grapevine,' which clung to the top of the British charts for six months.

In May, Blind Faith burst onto the rock scene, only to supernova a few short months later with Rick Grech, Stevie Winwood, and Eric Clapton flying off into brilliant splinter groups. 'Get Back' was released by the Beatles, and Humble Pie was formed by guitarist Peter Frampton and singer Steve Marriot. Led Zeppelin was beginning to prove to stubborn Britishers why they were so enormous in the U.S. And on July 5, 1969, in *Melody Maker's Album Supplement*, appeared a thumbnail review of a debut album – Elton John's *Empty Sky*:

People are predicting great things of Elton John,
a talented youth who plays piano, organ, electric piano
and harpsichord. It's a fine debut.

But that was about all the accolades Elton and Bernie would receive for the time being. *Empty Sky* whistled to the empty winds, and as far as sales went, it might as well have never been released.

As loose, unorganized, wild, free, and exuberant as any first album could be, *Empty Sky* was the first real professional collaboration of Bernie and Elton. Put together by the self-avowed amateur producer Steve Brown, *Sky* featured names which would become strikingly familiar to Elton John fans in the few short years to come. There was Caleb Quaye on drums, Tony Murray on bass, and Nigel Olsson playing drums on the cut called 'Lady, What's Tomorrow.'

Clive Frank did some whistling on a cut and operated the tape. Dave Larken sketched the bluish pen-and-ink portrait of Elton for the cover.

The title track, 'Empty Sky,' opened the album with an entire zoo of postpsychedelic sound effects – thumping congas, twanging bass à la the Stones' *His Satanic Majesty's Request*, giraffe bellows, lions in the bush, distortion, wind tunnels, and echo chambers. Somehow, though the song was beautifully controlled by the husky tones of the singer. It was intense, it was poetic, it was ambitious; the weird semitragic images of Taupin's verse seemingly materializing out of nowhere to paint 'Val Hala.' Taupin's image-landscape immediately countered the empty depression of the first song with a picture of a Teutonic paradise. Already Elton and Bernie were beginning to use their characteristic pattern – creating a lyrical problem caused by reality and then escaping from it into a dream ('You can come to Val Hala/in your own time'). It was very romantic. The rippling harpsichord painted a sonic picture of a never-never land while the electric piano added another dimension of other wordliness. But Elton's vocals never developed too far beyond the South Pacific style on the 'Val Hala' cut.

Some of the songs were forgettable, best remembered only as harbingers of the powerful ballads on *Elton John* and *Madman Across the Water*. Some of them were adolescent praises to their gods, the Beatles and the Stones, among others.

'Hymn 2000,' with its cushiony vocals, tinny piano, warbling flute, and family motif, tips its cap to *Sgt. Pepper's* 'Day in the Life.' Like many songs Elton would write in the future, it's about how to maintain strength in the midst of insanity, absurd relationships, and the social system. ('For soon they'll plough the desert. And God knows where I'll be/Collecting the submarine numbers/On the main street of the sea.')

'Sails' brings it all back to earthy waters. This cut has a fine funky blues-guitar line from Caleb and some hot chops from Elton's piano. 'Skyline Pigeon' was included on the disc, along with an exotic half-mythological, half-nightmare, 'The Scaffold.' For the grand finale, Elton, Bernie, and Steve topped the whole album with 'Gulliver Hay Chewed/Reprise.' Here, the hot guitar licks whipped up visual images into a whirlwind of emptiness and death: 'And Gulliver's gone with the dawn.' At this point the album's pace changes abruptly, twisting suddenly into a ragtime with boogying sax-and-guitar jam. Then the album quickly evolves into a weird medley of all the songs on the album, bordered by strange rushing and cacophonous sound effects. It was as if the engineer had gone beserk, turning up the sound volume higher and higher while the instruments ran amok in a mad series of flashbacks.

In the final analysis the LP had a new sound, made unique by the strange molding force of Elton's voice. It was a brilliant amateur production. All in all, an achievement Elton could never execute again, when, in his more sophisticated days, he chose Paul Buckmaster and Gus Gudgeon to map out his recorded terrain.

Few people had ever heard of *Elton John* or *Sky*. The first LP had passed virtually unnoticed except by a few attentive listeners in the United Kingdom and abroad. One of those sharp-eared discophiles, Eric Van Lustbader in New York, heard about the *Sky* album ordered it from Dick James Music in London and wrote a review comparing Elton's pioneering talent to that of the freshly born Chicago band. 'In the future,' he forecasted, 'the stars are going to be coming from England,' and, he said in parenthesis, 'Elton John will be huge.'

Elton John read that review, even while he was recording his next album. 'He freaked out,' related Lustbader, 'but he didn't take it seriously.' In the interim the star to be was still serving tea at Mill Music. And because his albums hadn't brought in a farthing, he took an extra job working eight hours a day in an import shop. 'It's a ball here,' Elton said from behind the counter. 'If I didn't want to be a recording star the best thing I could imagine would be to have a record store somewhere and serve behind the counter. These records just fascinate me,' he said, flashing back to the memory of the toddler Reggie Dwight, standing hypnotized by the endlessly spinning bright colors on the phonograph. 'The label, that's to me the magic of discs,' he explained. 'I mean, tapes are all right to take around with you, but there's no magic in watching a cassette tape.'

Elton and Bernie spent every moment in the studio trying to record and improve. Often they walked out of the studio at four in the morning, too excited to sleep or go home. They'd stroll over to Wimpy's bar to talk about the album and the rock scene. Elton was already an incorrigible disc collector, and he kept close track of what new albums were coming into the record shops. If the LPs were a day late, the two musicians would be crushed with disappointment. But then if they were the first to pick up the new Jefferson Airplane, they'd feel on top of the world. (Later Elton was to pay the price of stardom. He now simply ticked off the new releases as they appeared in the trade journals and had them shipped over. Some of the magic was lost in the ease fame brought with it.)

During those crazy sunrise periods, Elton and Bernie cut up the town in outrageous clothing. The self-conscious elf was beginning to let loose with a bit of his own unique humor, and he found himself beginning to put on wild costumes. Even Long John Baldry took note of the transformation and remarked to mutual acquaintances, 'You know, Elton [Reg] looks like he's sort of half-blind. I think it was yesterday or recently, he was wearing a green jacket with apples on it or cabbages or something. The trouble is, though, Reggie's got one of those figures where it doesn't matter if he spends millions of pounds on clothes [which he did begin to do, as a matter of fact, two years later] he still looks like a nun somehow, you know what I mean? Because he's got a long torso and tiny little short legs and a little tub and rear. It's not a balanced figure at all.'

'Yeah,' someone else returned. 'Everytime I see him, I think of an albino baboon.' That comment always was to remain a slight stab in the heart of our hero. 'I prefer to think I look like a human cheesecake,' he said aloofly in response. Elton was still madly dieting, alternating a strange citrus diet with wild cheesecake and strawberry splurges.

Those were creative times, though, despite the antics. Elton and Bernie's relationship began to grow and define itself. It was obvious that the Lincolnshire man's verses were, in some fateful way, necessary to Elton's composition. In songs like 'First Episode at Heinton,' the melody lines and rhythms climbed on the structure of Bernie's words like rose vines on high trellises. They gave Elton the narrowing discipline without which he couldn't shape his musical form.

As the twosome sat hunched over steaming coffee and the sun rose over the London towers, the two raked over their songs endlessly. 'I think "Hymn 2000" is really awful,' Elton said bluntly some time later about some of Bernie's favorite lyrics, 'and a couple of other tracks were pretty pretentious.' But when Bernie wasn't nearby, Elton would admit, 'He's got over being pretentious and he's got down to saying things very simply. He's finding his own way. After all, Bernie's not yet twenty-one. It's very good that Bernie's sentimental. And he's found his niche, and he doesn't churn things out. I really have to persuade him to write.' Bernie was rapidly becoming indispensable.

'I really don't know what's going on in Bernie's mind,' Elton admitted at one point. 'I ask him if a certain song is about a certain person or something like that, but I don't get any sense out of him.'

Bernie just shrugged his shoulders and wouldn't say. At other times, however, Elton believed he understood Bernie's words inside out. Bernie wrote only personal things. And because Elton knew him, when he received the lyrics in the mail, he knew exactly what the poet was talking about, what state of mind he was in. He knew what lady Bernie was involved with when he wrote the song.

But Bernie, like most artists, could not define or explain to anyone how he came up with his lyrics. Sometimes he simply flashed a title; it came to him like a neon sign in the city nights. Other times he would suddenly find himself whispering a line or two as he was driving along the winding roads of the Cotswolds. By the time he reached his cottage, the song might have been completely composed, and he'd rush inside to write it all down before it was forgotten.

Basically it took Bernie a remarkably short time to write a lyric. If he found himself spending more than an hour conjuring up a verse, he'd forget it and try something else. He never wanted to, as he put it, 'waste time.' It all had to be done at once. He lost interest if it didn't. Seldom did he write a song about a particular subject or person from scratch. Usually it was a first line or one somewhere in the middle or a title, then it came alive.

Elton, on the other hand, thought of himself as a music writer, a composer only. 'Not a lyrics writer. No, I can't do them. I know what I want to say, but when I try to write it down, it all comes out such – achhh – mush. But Bernie, no matter how he puts it down, it manages to come out beautifully, and my music takes off from there.'

For Bernie and Elton, physical proximity had nothing to do with their ability to work. They could be separated for six months, thousands of miles lying between them, and still write perfectly blended elements. Sometimes Bernie wrote lyrics in his wooded cottage in Lincolnshire, almost visualizing the melody in his mind. And sending them to Elton in London, he would be amazed when, six months later, he heard the lyrics. They would be set to music which was the *exact* melody he had in mind when he wrote the words. It was as if they had worked them out side by side; it was as if they were of *one* mind.

'When Taupin's barren we do nothing,' Elton later admitted. 'I can't do a thing,' he revealed in a husky voice, 'until Bernie's produced some lyrics.' What it all added up to was the startling recognition that Elton and Bernie were absolutely essential to each other's creative energies and talents.

CHAPTER 8

May, 1970.

'Things were really getting out of hand,' Steve Brown said to *Melody Maker* of the recording days of *Elton John*. 'And I just wasn't experienced enough to arrange and produce those albums.' Even though Elton protested, Steve convinced him to look for a more experienced man to arrange and spin the dials on his next LP – an album that would be crucial to Elton. Elton reluctantly took up his suggestion and began to hunt for a new producer.

'We asked the usual people,' said Elton, meaning George Martin, particularly, the wizard electrician who molded Beatle concepts into multilayered technical masterpieces. But Martin was going to be busy for five more weeks. Martin also stipulated that he'd arrange Elton's next LP only if he could produce as well, and only if it were done at Air London. That was too many stipulations for Elton.

'We waited,' said Elton, 'and then Tony Hall came over and said he had a bloke named Paul Buckmaster, who'd made *Sounds Nice*. We had nothing to lose, so we went round to see him.'

In a small flat inhabited by a vacuum cleaner and an electric clock with no dial, lay a cello, dust, and Paul Buckmaster, shivering in a dressing gown. Paul Buckmaster was quite thin, the strain of late hours and intense work in recording studios dug deeply into his dark young face.

Following the introductions, Buckmaster presented his qualifications as a producer. 'I see myself as what the

Establishment would term mad and in need of treatment,' he admitted to *Melody Maker*. 'In our world we're ready to realize that madness is in everyone,' continued the cello player who had brought his classical training to the progressive rock group, The Third Ear (called 'Turdies' by friends). 'Pop and rock are limiting things,' he discovered. 'Music is everywhere; and I believe in free music, as long as there's a fusion between the musicians.'

Elton and Steve played Paul a rough demo of 'Your Song.'

'I don't want to do it,' was the cello strummer's immediate response. 'I really don't want to touch it. It sounds too nice.' But before the visit was over, the young men began to come to an understanding. Paul, who characterized himself as 'a musician full stop,' played them some things he was working on and before they left the narrow room with the dialless clock, Paul and Elton had agreed to work together. 'And,' Paul added, 'I know a producer named Gus Dudgeon whom I feel comfortable working with.'

Elton and Steve took their songs over to Gus, a bespectacled fellow who looked as if he ought to be studying law instead of hanging out at rock dives and drafty studios. Elton was happy to meet him, having been considerably impressed by Dudgeon's arrangement and production of David Bowie's *Space Oddity*.

Elton and Steve played the rough demo of 'Your Song' for Gus just as they had for Paul. And like Paul, Gus warmed to the boys but wasn't too keen on their music. 'Eventually we got him down to it,' Elton said, 'and then we really worked the album out.'

The very first session Gus Dudgeon worked on laid the basic tracks for a cut called 'Take Me to the Pilot.' 'It just clicked from the start,' said Gus. 'After about four songs, I knew this was what I wanted to do.' As for the new arranger, Paul Buckmaster, Elton later commented, 'He's probably the most humble arranger I've ever met. Paul really didn't like what he did with "60 Years On." He reckoned it sounds like a thirties horror movie score. He was always apologizing for it, but his head's amazing. I know his head was way above what we were doing. But he enjoys doing my stuff,' Elton continued, 'and if he stops getting enjoyment he'll stop arranging.'

It seemed as if *Elton John* was the album the U.S. had been waiting for. Back in New York, Eric Van Lustbader, the critic who had gushed happily over Elton's *Empty Sky*, was now working at *Cashbox* magazine, a music trade paper. In the merry month of May, Eric was called upstairs to the Dick James Music headquarters which coincidentally happened to be located in the same building as *Cashbox*. David Rossner, the head of DJM in the U.S., wanted Lustbader to hear a new single he had just received from London.

Eric ran upstairs, not waiting for the elevator, and arrived at the moment Rossner was switching on the console. Out of the speakers spilled a rich chorus. 'It's called "Border Song"!' Lustbader exclaimed before Rossner could open his mouth. 'And that's Elton John.' Rossner fell off his chair. 'How'd you know?' he asked.

'Because I have *Empty Sky* – it's a great album. And I knew Elton was building up to something like this.'

'Border Song' was a smash hit in America, burning the westerners' ears like musical wildfire. The album sold out in thousands of stores the very day it was placed on the racks.

'I knew it was going to hit,' said Lustbader later. 'It's the same quality that turned me on to Cat Stevens and the Beatles. It's an awareness of something there that hasn't been there in music before. It's rare to find a person who creates his own form of music. That's what Elton John has done.'

From the opening notes of 'Your Song' through 'First Episode at Heinton,' to the brooding chords of 'The King Must Die,' melodies and verse flowed together out of some pure wellspring of emotion, seemingly unrehearsed and uncomplicated by holding back or revision. The cover portrait, executed by David Larkham, revealed in semi-profile an intense, somber Elton staring into the shadows. And every tune on the disc inside created a musical mood, a landscape unavailable to almost every sense.

After the upbeat offering of 'Your Song,' Elton began to plunge into tense dark states. Each song had its own particular form of tension and anxious questioning. In 'I Need You to Turn To,' the harpsichord set the private space where the slow undercurrents of strings carried the stark vocal. 'You are nailed to my love in many lonely nights . . . My reason for living was for loving you.' The song ends in notes falling like tears, heavily, but with delicate string support. (Many interpretations of this song were sent to Elton in the years to come, but the piano man had forgotten it by then.)

The next cut, 'Take Me to the Pilot,' abruptly jumped into a totally opposite mood, a strange, almost manic state, evoked by guitars and piano playing wildly at cross-currents. Another one of Elton-Taupin's strangely am-

Elton does deep knee bends on 'Bennie and the Jets'

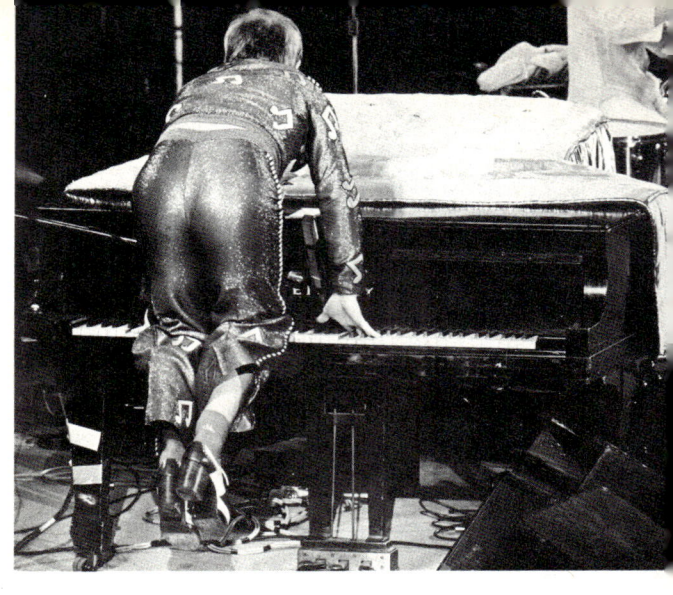

Anti-gravity pulls Mr John away from the keyboards

Elton looks to Bernie Taupin for more lyrics

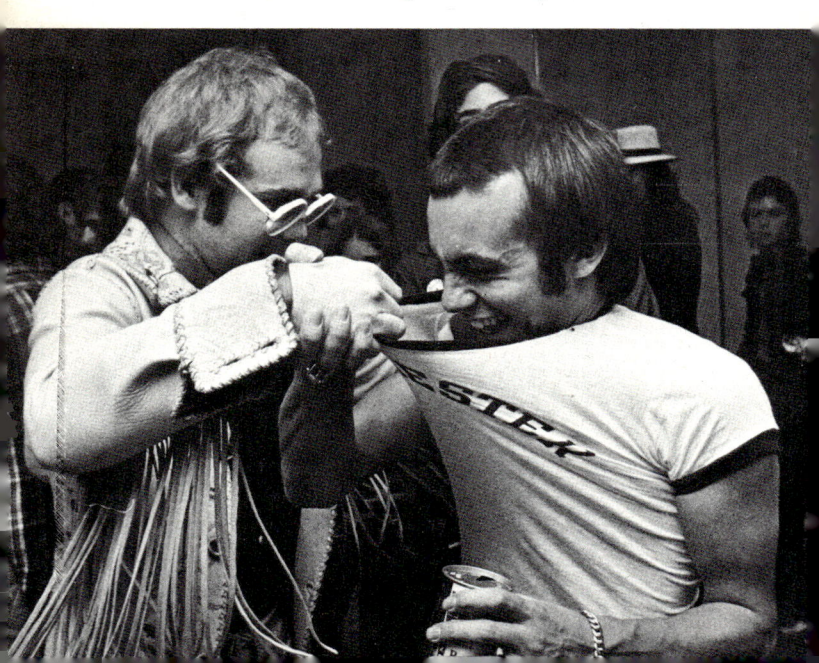

No one has more fun at an Elton John concert than the piano-pounder in the winged saddle shoes

Elton John at the Santa Monica Civic Centre in 1970

Elton helps burn down the mission
in his plaid safari shirt

Elton in leotards and Fillmore team T-shirt at the Santa Monica Civic Centre early in his star flight

Elton is starry-eyed at a press conference at Universal Studios in Los Angeles in 1971. Flanking him are Bernie and Dee

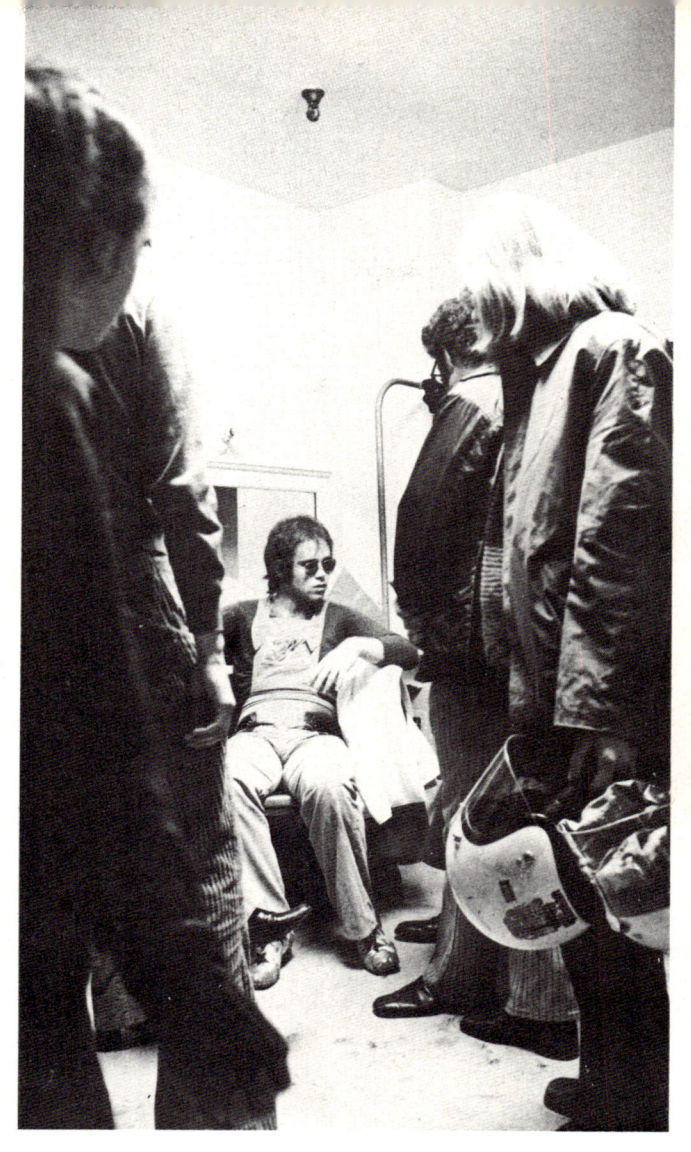

After pouring an incredible outburst
of raw power over the audience
at Royce Hall at U C L A in 1971,
Elton recovers backstage with biking friends

Elton and furry friend, given to him by poet partner Bernie Taupin

Dee Murray, Nigel Olsson, Elton and Davey Johnstone – four guys on a bandwagon

Elton spies on dinner-jacketed piano player at the Los Angeles Forum

Elton in boas at the Hollywood Bowl in 1973

Elton presses the flesh on ecstatic fans at the Hollywood Bowl in 1973

Astronaut and Rocket man: Nigel and Dee peer at Apollo 15 command module flyer, Al Worden, while a striped-suited Elton and astounded Davey hum a few bars of 'Take Me to the Pilot'

Elton's crocodile rocks on his electric piano at the Hollywood Bowl concert in 1973

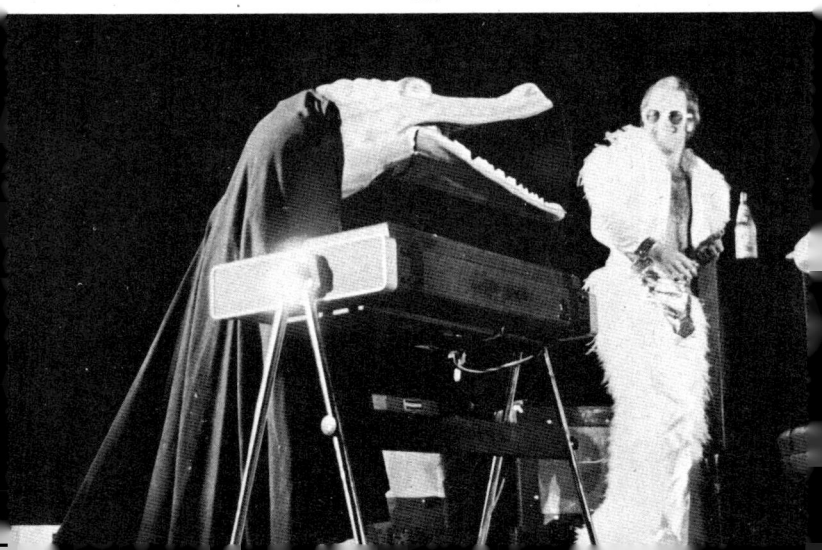

Elton takes a dry run in his bathtub. His bathroom is reputed to be the most lavish in the world

Princess Margaret, Lord Snowden, and the Prince of Pop

Josie Pollack and Elton's drummer Nigel Olsson with EJ at the launching of Rocket Records

Elton with his manager, John Reid
celebrate the formation of
Rocket Records

Elton balances on one platform,
five fingers, and a boogie beat

Elton with his Faces friend, Ronnie Wood

biguous songs, it seemed to be about a prisoner's demand for freedom, a furious gesture in the face of some cosmic jailer. And 'Pilot' was followed by still another odd song, 'First Episode at Heinton.' The spectacular use of heavy orchestration built up an uncanny, almost cinematic (Wuthering Heights) emotional climate: lost love, passing years, loneliness. The high octave strings, rippling harps, and moog wails built up a landscape you could almost walk into. The song might have dissolved into a tearjerker, however, had it not been for the strange half-tone progressions, the fleeting images and superb arrangement.

It was not the music of a young man. Nor was '60 Years On,' with its buzzing sound effects and melancholy Spanish guitar. The down mood of the LP was given relief by 'Border Song,' though, complete with soaring gospel chorus. But the album ended on notes of heavy cynicism with 'The King Must Die.'

Several years later, when she was asked which of her son's hit albums was her favorite, Sheila Dwight chose the second, *Elton John*. 'I love that album because some of the tracks are so sad. I love sad music – and I think Elton is a terribly sad person. I remember I used to sit there crying my eyes out when he was a child.'

Elton John gave the critics some entirely new music to chew on. 'The music on this album is so eclectic it at once strains the bonds of previous frames of reference and requires new ones to encompass it,' opined one reviewer.

'Heavy intellectual music,' declared another, 'intensified by the arrangements of Paul Buckmaster and the production of Gus Dudgeon.'

'Paul Buckmaster is a damned genius,' raved an underground critic in London, about the cello-playing arranger.

'*Elton John* is an album of almost primitive beauty,' exclaimed another critic in May, 1970. 'Elton John is a brilliant composer and a fine singer. Paul Buckmaster has incredibly sympathetic arrangements. This is an album to hear right now.' The raves avalanched. Elton was ecstatic, but he was taken by surprise. Such acclaim was hard to handle. But he was ready for more. He decided it was time for Elton John to go public.

On April 21, 1970, Elton John was booked to appear on British television, a program called *Top of the Pops*, which was by far the most influential televised music program in existence. An appearance on *Top of the Pops* could make you into a superstar overnight – or break you to pieces between station identification.

Elton needed a brilliant band. In comparing the dangers of instant stardom on *Top of the Pops*, instead of a slower, surer way to get recognition, Elton said, '*Top of the Pops* doesn't give anybody any idea of what you can do. In fact, it gives them a totally wrong impression.'

Joined on *Top of the Pops* for the first time by bassist Dee Murray and his drummer friend Nigel Olsson, Elton unleashed an uplift in performance, powerful enough to make the critics purr. 'It's nice to see Cat Stevens and Elton John providing the British answer to Neil Young and Van Morrison,' they touted. But Elton hadn't yet let loose with his real power.

What a cultural shock it was going to be – especially for the insulated music fans who thought Elton was one of those moody soloists hunched over a piano like a brooding James Taylor – to behold the resplendent Elton decked to his ears in all his flamboyant lamé and platforms. Joined by

Dee and Nigel, Elton was beginning to let his imagination carry him to new extremes of show biz antics, moves that would drive old, venerable rock freaks to a new pitch of frenzied boogie-mania. For the first time since the Bill Haley motion picture triumph *Rock Around the Clock* played at the now-demolished Queen's Cinema in 1956, the kid in the crowd felt the urge to take up a knife and slash at a tip-up seat, when he was swept up in an Elton John performance. Reason usually prevailed, though, and the hysterically happy youth danced on the upholstery (instead of slicing it) along with several thousand other possessed fans. That was the impact of Elton John and his band.

The live act, including Elton's famous jumping business, started accidentally. Elton was scheduled to play an outdoor festival in Halifax at the Crumlin Festival. 'How's that for a name – the Crumlin Festival,' Elton quipped to his band as they arrived in their new heated and air-conditioned van. 'It's freezing cold up here, man,' commented Dee, flinging his arms around. 'I don't know how we're going to keep our bums from freezing off,' Nigel muttered, shaking. The three were beginning to joke about how they could keep warm during their act up on the exposed stage when someone asked, 'Hey boss, you've always been into Jerry Lee Lewis-type acts, haven't you?' And Elton suddenly had a brain flash.

'If I start jumping about, not even caring what I'm doing, at least I'll keep my ass warm.' So he did, kicking out the piano bench, flinging himself under the piano, jumping up on its top, playing the keys with his boots, with his teeth, with the top of his bobbing head. The crowd went absolutely gazonkers. No one had ever ever been so totally outrageous.

'Let's keep it from now on,' the sweat-drenched piano man gasped after the last wild applause died away. 'The audience is getting a kick out of it and so do I. And that's what it's all about,' he added happily, 'the fact that some pudgy little guy in outrageous gear can get up on a piano and wiggle his ass off and people think that's sexy. Well, I think it's a hoot. But as far as the people behind the Elton John show? Well there's only one thing behind me, and I'm sitting on it.'

But almost before the British audiences knew what the Elton John craze was all about, the stubby maestro, accompanied by Dee and Nigel, took off to conquer the Americas. But they had to be pushed before they would take the transatlantic plunge.

The *Elton John* album, while soaring on the American charts, bombed in England. It came out and died, going into the BBC charts at forty-five (there are fifty places in the BBC listing) and slipping out again. The people at Dick James Music were surprised because they assumed it would at least stay in the charts, with its special orchestration and musical effects. But it died. Elton, meanwhile, didn't want to go on the road. He didn't want to know what was happening to the record. But the DJM bigwigs insisted: 'You have to go on the road and promote it.' Thus Elton prepared to go to the U.S. because the record company insisted.

Elton only wanted to go to the U.S. to look at the fabulous record stores which were rumored to exist like castles of Oz on the western shore of the Atlantic. 'Also,' he added, 'it was either go to the U.S. or Jeff Beck was going to join us. But it turned out we would have had to join Jeff Beck. So we went to the States.'

Elton, Dee, and Nigel roared across the Atlantic to make a smashing debut tour. In September, 1970, the British press reported that Elton was selling out houses across the western nation, grossing fifty thousand dollars in one week. *Elton John* was being immediately re-pressed for instant shipping to the U.S. while Bell Records was covering 'Take Me to the Pilot' by a group called Birds of a Feather – a new all-girl vocal outfit. At the same time Bernie and Elton were rumored to be writing a film script for a Lewis Gilbert film called *Friends* to be released by Paramount.

Elton kicked off his first great U.S. tour by opening at the renowned Troubadour club in Los Angeles. His West Coast PR man, Norman Winter, actually rolled out the red carpet, by picking up the entire Elton John entourage in an authentic English bus, fully equipped with double-deckers and Guinness Stout advertisements and a bright scarlet paint job. Elton emerged blinking from the plane; he was sporting a furry beard (though shorn locks), work pants, and he turned as red as the bus with embarrassment when he caught sight of his 'limousine.'

The bus prank was one that Elton would blush over for years to come. He actually couldn't believe such an embarrassing thing was happening to him – being carted through L.A. in a huge red barn of a vehicle. Elton was a practical jokester, but Winter's ebullient gesture had simply gone too far. On the way from the airport the entire group had been bent double trying to crawl into a crouch and hide below the windowline. Violent thoughts of what he was going to do to his publicity man might have raced through the elfin thumper's mind as he squatted in the careening omnibus. But, naturally, he said nothing to Winter about his gaucherie. Elton could never be rude to people. He would rather go through with it – suffer inside and smile and laugh, rather than be nasty to well-meaning admirers.

But that night Elton's show at the Troubadour was, according to all who were there, one of the greatest opening nights in Los Angeles rock. While the well-acoustic space hummed with the enormous crowd of expectant musicians, movie stars, and press, and the liquor flowed in torrents from the bar, the air was charged with a new electricity. Elton appeared on stage, and pandemonium reigned. During 'Take Me to the Pilot,' Odetta, to everyone's joy, jumped up in the back row and danced, strutting and twirling that famous huge body around like a big-mama cyclone. Leon Russell, supreme among Elton's rock 'n' roll gods, sat near the front and made Elton so nervous he almost blew the last number, 'Burn Down the Mission.' But the audience gasped and clapped every time he began to play another cut off the album.

While Elton mulled over the present and future, his agent at the time, Jerry Heller, was extremely impressed, even ecstatic. Heller, at his agency, Chartwell, had booked stars of such magnitude as Donovan and Eric Clapton, but on that day he viewed Elton John as a new phenomenon. 'It usually takes cross-country tours to establish an artist,' he detailed. 'But Elton is such an excellent composer and forceful personality that he's going to do it in two dates.'

Not only were the native Californians flipping out over the bespectacled ivories-tickler, forty-eight hours after the Troubadour opening, blond-tressed superstar, Leon Russell himself called Elton over to his house to jam. Elton's stubby little body went into instant rigor mortis with fear and awe. He might have had visions of himself being tied down to the piano while the accomplished Russell raced his fingers up and down the keyboard, saying, 'This is how to play the piano.' Elton worried as he sped down the thruways to the Oklahoma-born piano player's canyon retreat. Leon turned out, of course, to be very pleasant and the next day the Los Angeles *Times*, to top off Elton's dizzying amazement, hailed the myopic thumper as the first rock superstar of the seventies.

It was Elton's first tour, a first tour unprecedented in rock 'n' roll history. 'It was the week of the Million Handshakes,' Elton quipped in *Rolling Stone*. 'The Eddie Duchin Story or How Dis Boy Is a Genius.'

After the tornado-whipping assault of the Western Hemisphere Elton returned to the land of tea-sippers, pekoe-boilers, and Lipton-lovers and was propositioned to do a film. 'It was sort of a black comedy affair,' the tiny piano whacker commented. Paramount asked Elton to star in *Harold and Maude*, the story of a twenty-year-old who fell in love with an eighty-year-old woman. It featured a script by Colin/Higgins of UCLA film school fame, and directed by Hal Ashby of *The Landlord*. But Elton was not interested and let the opportunity drop without comment. At the same time, Paramount approached him and Bernie with a film score for the Paramount release, *Friends*. The duo was intrigued with the film possibilities, and even before he had finished reading through the first half of the script, Bernie had penned three songs – 'the three songs that were actually written for the script,' he explained, 'and the other songs were things we'd just had about and Gilbert the director stuck them in.'

'All the *Friends* stuff was done in three weeks,' added Elton. 'It was such a panic.'

After *Friends* was filmed, edited, and in the can, Paramount insisted that the Taupin-John sound track be released. Elton protested. 'I don't want them to release a sound track with three songs on it and fill it out with the sounds of garbage being dumped and motorists peeing by the sides of lakes,' complained the irate piano tuner, to *Rolling Stone* as he grew more outspoken with every day of increasing stardom. 'So we got two spare songs, "Honeyroll" and "Can I Put You On?" They put them on the track during the transistor-radio sequence. We put them on as a bonus, really. I regret that because, fuck, I would have wanted to put them on our own album.'

The music people and film people didn't hit it off. When Bernie and Elton were down at Olympic cutting the sound track, film people continually dropped by to command the session. 'Oh, you should do this,' one cameraman might say, 'and you shouldn't do that.'

It was like working in a factory on a Vega assembly line. Or in a computerized sweatshop. They had to write exactly forty seconds of music and if they didn't write forty, if they wrote forty-five, it was a disaster. Elton and Bernie found the film people more arrogant than dukes in the House of Lords.

CHAPTER 9

But soon the duo's annoyance was swept away in the torrential response to their third album. Released in Britain in the middle of October, 1970, *Tumbleweed Connection* cinched Elton's position as 'Mistah Superfunk!' Record freaks gathered in all corners of the United Kingdom to discuss the blond bomber's newest package. All over London, youths peered at the 1980s Mississippi River-boat cover while they gazed at the photographs and lyric sheets on the inside of the album. Said one tousled-hair aficionado in a dimly lit milk bar in Soho, 'Elton John does it better than people like the Bramletts or Joe Cocker because he's funky without copying it off of soul exclusively. There are all sorts of influences in this music.'

'Yeah,' added another kid who'd joined the gang huddled over the *Tumbleweed* album his friends had spread on the table among the fish and chips and crumbling cakes. 'He's coming off the downer he was on in the Elton John album too. I dig the machine-gun piano on "Ballad of an Unknown Gun," and the funky guitar and soul choruses too. Nigel's right on top of the beat, too, doing that typical Olsson thing, giving the impression of laying back.'

'That's Dusty Springfield on the back-ups,' added a waitress who was eavesdropping on the conversation as she served the two blokes their fish and chips. 'But I like "Come Down in Time" with its bits of Spanish guitar and *cor anglais*. The cut off is amazing.'

'My, my, you can say that again,' winked the chums. 'Did you know that "Country Comfort" is really Rod Stewart's? He did it on *Gasoline Alley* first. Elton has prettier harmonies on the chorus, though. It's a real send-up with all that steel guitar and all.'

'Love Song', the only lyric not penned by Bernie, had a distinct Crosby, Stills, and Nash sound, as did the opening phrases of 'My Father's Gun.' But 'Where to St. Peter' escaped the western fantasy world to spring into the pure melodic and lyrical tightness that the best of Elton and Bernie's songs always possessed. The meaning and the musical phrasing was absolutely perfect – the image of the singer as a blue canoe carried down a long drunken river was conveyed by the leaping treble line. 'Burn Down the Mission,' the closing cut, began gently enough, but evolved into an all-time tear-up as Gus Dudgeon's arrangement climaxed Elton's insanely triumphant piano. 'Mission' seemed the closest thing to a political protest statement Bernie was to write, and it brought the house, if not the mission, down every time they performed it. But actually 'Mission' was just another fantasy song; the mission burner was no Mark Rudd, but a loony pyromaniac, and in the end they came and took him away. Like the rest of the songs on *Tumbleweed*, though, 'Mission' glowed with the fire of active fantasy making. It was the dynamic duo's total fascination for the America's long-gone West that made the album a cut above most other country and western offshoots.

Tumbleweed was released in the U.S. in January, while Elton John was still soaring high in the charts, *Tumbleweed* rolled straight in at No. 25 and within weeks streaked upwards to join *Elton* in the first five places.

But even before *Tumbleweed* had blown into the U.S. Elton, Dee, and Nigel began packing up their gear and swooped off into the setting sun to catch the American fans just as *Tumbleweed* broke on the western shores. It was the second U.S. tour in six months. *Tumbleweed* had not yet hit, but the crowds went crazy at every concert, giving the troll and his band standing ovations during and at the end of every show. It was a major tour, covering all the big cities, and it was extremely strenuous. One night, Seattle, the next, Minneapolis, the next, Phoenix (the home of the snake-flinging Alice Cooper), then on to St. Louis, Dallas, and Baton Rouge. On a rare night off, the entire troupe would collapse in their Holiday Inns, too exhausted to turn off the flickering TV sets.

In the Los Angeles area alone, Elton gave five concerts – San Bernardino, Riverside, Anaheim, Santa Monica, and UCLA – an unprecedented number. In Chicago, Mr. John had to be hoisted in the air by the police, his plump little body zooming in across the heads of the screaming crowds. Bob Dylan came out of hiding to see him, and his all-time idols the Band invited themselves to an East Coast gig.

Watching the show from backstage, Bernie was at first red from embarrassment for his tiny twin. 'Oh, no!' he thought as the chubby form began to leap about in the red and yellow lights while the audiences screamed and cheered. In a few weeks, however, Bernie began to understand Elton's personal form of frenzy. Bernie began to make sudden surprise appearances on stage himself.

The Elton John band was ripping up the United States. Leon Russell, remembering the Troubadour, called in a request. He wanted Bernie to write a song for him. 'I've never written anything specifically for another singer before,' Bernie admitted almost hesitantly, 'but we're going to play with Leon at the Fillmore East in New York. He's got a good band with a couple of chick singers. We're planning to do a gig where we do our respective acts and then go on stage together.'

It was a magnificent plan, complete with duelling pianos and two blond firebombs, one tall and flowing maned, the other panda sized.

It was the night of the Fillmore Concert that Elton John was going to meet one of the most important men in his life. Backstage in the dark, smoke-filled dressing rooms of Bill Graham's New York showcase, a tousle-haired man appeared wrapped in a dark green trench coat. In the years to come this man would execute Elton's greatest show-business fantasies.

His name was Ron Delsener. He was a small wiry guy who made his start writing athlete's foot powder commercials for TV. After conceiving a famous advertising character called 'The Beloved Herring Mayven,' Delsener sold Rheingold beer the idea of staging free concerts for New Yorkers in Central Park. The plan was so successful Delsener thrilled New York by putting on the historical free Barbra Streisand concert that attracted one hundred thousand people.

In a few years Delsener was the best, and the classiest of independent promoters in the business. The night of the Fillmore, Delsener had come all the way downtown to hear an unknown from England named Elton John. 'Howard Rose, who's Elton's L.A. agent and his friend,' Delsener said later in a tough New York accent, 'played me this record called *Tumbleweed Connection* from England. It hadn't come out in the States, but I listened to it and said, "Gee, that's great. Who is it?" "Elton John," he said, "and first we're gonna put him in the Fillmore, because he wants to play a rock palace first. Then we'll do a class hall."

'I thought he was a tasteful artist,' continued Delsener as telephones rang and show-business types rambled through the small office. 'He doesn't have to play dark basements like that to get to the kids. So I went to see him at the Fillmore, just to say hello. The band was sitting back there in the Fillmore dressing rooms. They were kind of slumped over, looking messy. There was a lot of noise going on, a lot of people, kind of like a warm-up before a prize fight. Apart from all these people, Elton John slumped over with one hand on his chin. He got up and gave me one of those nice smiles of his and struck me as a very with-it person. He was dressed in a great style; fun and campy. He had lots of appeal, and I knew I'd hit it off with him. And the rest of the guys in the band were great too. I knew Elton and I would put on a great concert one day, and next year Carnegie Hall turned out to be it.'

The Fillmore concert was a triumphant pinnacle of the tour. The Band, Elton's all-time favorite group, was there to catch the show.

'Bernie was shaking with fear,' Elton told the British in a transatlantic telephone call, 'but the Band was really sweet and we talked for three hours.'

'Then came the most incredible thing,' Elton continued a few days later as the after-effect of the high slowly brought him back down to earth. 'Because after the Fillmore gig we said good-bye to the Band and set off for

Philadelphia while they went in the opposite direction, upstate New York. We played a fantastic gig in Philly and when we got to our dressing rooms afterward the entire Band was there. They'd put their show forward a couple of hours and flew down to see our gig!' Elton was thrilled.

The piano man played the *Tumbleweed* album for them, and, he raved. 'They went berserk. It was such a compliment I couldn't believe it. They asked us to go back to Woodstock with them to record at Big Pink, and when Robbie Robertson asked us to write a song for him – well, I think Bernie was a bit embarrassed because Robbie is his current idol.'

The entire tour was filled with such high points. Elton was just beginning to experience the breathtaking freedom of stardom. The first effect instant fame had on the pudgy hero was to drive him wild over clothes. As his stage acts got wilder and wilder, so did his costumes. At Santa Monica Elton wore a Mick Jagger top hat, cape, and purple jump suit. During 'Burn Down the Mission,' he kicked away the piano stool, ripped off his jump suit, and finished the song with an incredible series of giant bunny kicks in purple Danskin pantyhose. The crowd in Elton's words, 'went mental.'

'What with these ridiculous clothes, he's becoming a blooming comedian,' commented Dee.

'But I never wanted to be flash,' Elton objected. 'I'm very antiswish in a show-biz thing. But the clothes are me,' he admitted. 'Before, I was always fat and had to buy clothes that were awful. So when I lost weight that meant I could get into things. Since then I've always been outrageously dressed. I always wanted to dress like Mick Jagger – outrageous. So now I am. It's part of the fun. I'm having a laugh and sending everybody up,' he chuckled as he straightened the Donald Duck button on his pink and orange Bobby Brooks T-shirt.

Some of Elton's stranger costumes were the brainstorms of a tiny seamstress named Maxine who accompanied them on the American tour. The miniature blond designer who was always cheerful, comforting, and bubbling over with exorbitant ideas, Maxine was the light of the band. She spent a lot of time with the poet Bernie, and many friends commented on the transformation taking place in the bard from Lincolnshire.

'Bernie could be very moody,' explained Eric Van Lustbader when they were in New York. 'Moody in a real sense, not talking even to his closest friends for days at a time. After he got involved with Maxine he wasn't moody like that nearly as often or as intensely.'

Fate continued to shine upon Elton John during this tour. Opportunities fell at his feet like overripe fruit from the orchard of fortune. Even as *Elton* and *Tumbleweed* bounced around in stratospheres of Top Ten, and *Friends* entered the Top Forty, Elton was cutting a live album. All of England was following their piano-thumping ambassador's progress.

'Elton John Makes History with Live Radio Show,' was typical of the headlines in the British music weeklies. 'The first time it's happened in ages.' The album was consequently titled with the historic date *11-17-70*.

At WABC radio there was a man who was an incorrigible Elton John freak. At every opportunity he badgered Elton to do a live radio concert because he wanted to instigate live concerts on the air in New York. The first time he approached Elton and Bernie, they promptly turned him down. But the second time he knocked on their door he promised he'd put the duo in a recording studio instead of the chambers of WABC. Elton and Bernie finally agreed.

The studio was the famous A&R Studios on Seventh Avenue. They did it one evening with a hundred people in its small rooms and it went out on the air. Elton didn't know at the time it was going on eight-track. As far as he was concerned it was just going out over the air in good two-track stereo. Of course there were millions of people sitting at home taping it for a bootleg. But it was a superb tape, the best Elton had ever done.

Elton at first was stubbornly against a live album, and he had no intention of putting the WABC tapes on plastic. But when he listened to the eight-track, he softened a bit. The sounds were dynamite.

It was also a time when some fans were buying his record and others were coming to his rave-up concerts. But the two weren't always getting together. Many of the vinyl listeners thought Elton was a brooding man on stage, fainting after every fourth number. And the band wasn't getting much of a reputation either. The names Nigel Olsson and Dee Murray meant little or nothing to one who had not seen them blazing away before the spotlights. It was with these thoughts in mind that Elton was won over to releasing the broadcast as a kind of bootleg album – an authorized bootleg. His real spirit would be exposed and Nigel and Dee would get some money off it.

When *11-17-70* was released, it sounded like a legitimate bootleg with a low-key packaging medium and an almost documentary flavor.

Elton was ecstatic about the album he had so reluctantly

released. It was the result of a single recording moment, rather than the product of six dates of gigging sessions. Many live LPs were the result of getting a truck to follow a band to two or three dates, so that they could choose the best tracks out of a wide selection. Elton's was totally immediate, truly the capturing of a single live experience. And it was all unpremeditated.

CHAPTER 10

All of a sudden Elton John seemed in demand by everyone! He received invitations to parties, openings, and TV specials. On the *Andy Williams Show* he was scheduled to appear with one of his boyhood idols, Ray Charles. 'It was the most frightening experience of my life,' confessed the new superstar. 'I was petrified, but Ray Charles turned out to be very nice and we got on fine.' The accolades tumbled around his ears like an avalanche of roses. 'I don't think I can be more popular than I am now,' he commented daringly a few weeks later. But the real fame was yet to come.

In the midst of all this glory, Elton John was growing homesick. 'I haven't seen England all this year,' he complained, a little forlornly for a superstar. 'I'm looking forward to getting home December 12.' Elton arrived home to be with his mum, Sheila, for Christmas, but there was no rest for the bouncy pop star. Immediately upon his return he was scheduled to perform as many as five gigs a week, doing shows at the Roundhouse, on the road, and in the suburbs.

Strangely, inevitably though, the tide of good luck was beginning to turn against the elfin wonder-boy. Elton was booked at the Royal Festival Hall in a giant extravaganza. He was to play, backed by a thirty-five piece symphony orchestra.

The show was a disaster. The press screamed, 'Elton John has shown what a musical dwarf he really is.'

After that, there were more gigs and more snipes from the press. He was reviewed in *Melody Maker's* 'Caught In The Act.'

> 'Elton John was as hot as a docker's armpit, complex musically, ingenious, but musically and lyrically too similar, . . . It was sad, the man, this living myth, darling of the Americans, the ultimate local boy makes good, struggling like a pygmy center half with just 7,000 of his own people.

The press, it seemed, was out to get him.

Meanwhile, Bernie married the band's tiny seamstress, Maxine, 'My inspiration,' he called her. He promptly took off to the American wilderness to realize his dreams by fishing up and down the Mississippi River and camping in the West. In the midst of all this, while the press was alternately praising and damning him, Elton tried to prepare cuts for a new album and an itinerary for a new tour. The pressure was closing in on him, though. The crowning blow fell in the south of France.

Every New Year, by the side of the azure Mediterranean in the resort town of Cannes, the music industry holds an enormous gala convention replete with luxury hotel suites, magnificent banquets, liquor, mink-lined limousines, champagne parties, and all-night entertainment. MIDEM was where the shiny-suited businessmen of the music industry, the hustlers, publicity folk, radio people, and stringers gathered for their annual meetings. Billion-dollar deals were made and sealed by poolside and beach. A banker's holiday for the stock exchange of the music world, MIDEM was the climax to a year's hectic wheeling and dealing. And every night there was an especially exciting rock 'n' roll act to kick off the evening's celebration. January, 1971, the opening group was Eric Burden; War followed, and Elton John topped the bill.

The day after the MIDEM opening, however, newspapers sprang the shocking tidings, 'Eric Wars on Elton!' The previous night Eric Burden had literally blasted Elton away from the stage in a 'staggering display of selfishness and arrogance,' snarled *Melody Maker*. Elton and Eric, Great Britain's representatives at MIDEM, both had been allotted fourteen minutes each. But Burden and War roared away for an astounding one hour and ten minutes. Burden played continuously with no gaps between the songs, refusing to leave the stage despite the incessant and furious pleas from the organizers and the furious shouts from Elton. The curtain finally fell and the emcee announced Elton John. But Burden, undaunted, continued to blast on behind the curtain, the emcee's words being drowned out by the wailing brass and loud guitars. Having at last come to the end of his tether, Elton stomped out of the theater in a rage!

But that was not the end of Elton's Cannes jinx. Somebody persuaded him to return and do the second show the next night. He did the last number, the rock 'n' roll medley. And before they finished it, the curtain came down. Elton was reported in *Melody Maker* as spluttering, his fury rising even higher 'The French can't organize a piss-up in a brewery.' At this point the musical troll's ire got the best of him; like a tiny bull in a ring, he sprang from behind the curtain, grabbed the mike and bellowed to the bewildered audience, 'Whoever organized this fucking thing is a fucking idiot.' The entire audience cheered and clapped and Elton stalked off the stage.

There had been one other French experience, too, an earlier tour Elton did not find amusing to remember. The first time he, Dee, and Nigel had played together had been in the land of the Gauls and the natives had booed and thrown cabbages. Norman Granz had been the promoter and had been terribly upset. And the French, too, streamed up after the show in tears to apologize for their people.

On that first tour Elton had played on stage for an hour, stubbornly enduring the audience. Then he fled, leaving the stage to the star Sergio Mendes. Surely *he'd* go over big. But no, Mendes went on with waves and cheers and within fifteen minutes was receiving hisses and boos. Maybe it was only the French way of having an evening out on the town. They hurled everything at the performers – cigarette packs, panties, pictures of the Victorian and Albert Museum. It wasn't as if the musical troll hated the French: he loved their food, wine, and romantic Paris.

The pressure, though, was getting to him. He had already been on the verge of a nervous breakdown, and before the Cannes debacle he had been forced to cancel three British dates: Hull, Southampton, and Loughborough. He had arrived in the south of France gulping a doctor's regimen of vitamins, and he shook like a leaf. The doctor had warned him severely that he was on the edge of collapse. After MIDEM it happened.

He was feeling rotten, he had admitted to friends. It could only have been the strain of all those weeks. So much had happened at once, the elfin piano man was confused and exhausted. After all, he had never wanted to go on the road in the first place. Why did he leave Bluesology, if not to concentrate on making records and perhaps venture into producing? But there he was turning into a touring vegetable once again.

Elton's mind was whirling and his body was battered and worn. By the middle of the American tour his hands were excruciatingly painful. They bled every night, and the nails were broken. Then, once the skin hardened up it began to split under the jackhammer pressure of his keyboard pounding. By the time he got back to England, Elton was afraid his hands were ruined. Everything was moving much too quickly. At the exact same time a year earlier, Elton John had been a clerk in a record shop.

Time, they say, is relative, and for Elton, a year, like a minute or an hour, could be a long period of time. But for Elton the past year had been a whirlwind, a volcano that had erupted him into the lava of critical prominence. In that one year two or three albums recorded and released on the Uni label were certified gold (*Elton John* and *Tumbleweed Connection*) and the third, *11-17-70*, was due for certification any minute.

The elf's three singles, 'Your Song,' 'Border Song,' and 'Friends,' all made their mark on the top charts in the course of the amazing twelve-month period Elton and Bernie were showered with bucketfuls of critical praise. At the apex of that period, Elton announced an imminent summer LP release, this one to be called *Madman Across the Water*. 'It's going to be quite orchestrated,' described Elton, 'and it may be the last one we do with Paul Buckmaster, more like *Elton John* than *Tumbleweed Connection*.'

In April, just before the summer of *Madman*, the chunky, short-haired, pop star with the sun-colored bug-eyed glasses packed up his gear, rallied his boys, and set off for the Colonies once again. This time the high-energy ball of rock fire couldn't be stopped. He provoked a ten-week long plague of pop hysteria that climaxed with Elton being dubbed the Rock King of the Seventies.

On May 29, 1971, *Melody Maker* erroneously reported that Elton had fallen flat on his face on his second American tour, and that Elton's career was as dead as a doorknob. Americans were outraged, especially the music-business people who saw Elton as a breath of fresh air and a financial bonanza. One of the grateful Yanks was Bill Graham. The British pop weekly that had printed the incorrect report received a letter postmarked from a well-known rock concert hall in New York's lowest East Side:

> The report that Elton John was dead in the USA is not true. Elton John was alive and well at the Fillmore East. He sold to five packed houses in April, which were sold out five weeks in advance and we returned 6,000 mail order envelopes. I consider Elton one of the truly great entertainers working today.
>
> signed,
> Bill Graham

In one year, 1971, he had toured America, Japan and Australia. 'I turned up like a plate of jelly after that,' Elton confessed. 'It's true I was overworked, but we were so knocked out that people wanted us, and we said yes to everything.'

The prize for least pleasant experiences, however, went

to the island continent of Australia. When the rockets arrived in Perth they were invited to a reception by the mayor of Perth. But they were so tired by the endless plane ride that they ran to him and asked if they could postpone the event until the next day. Fine. That night on TV broke the shocking news: 'Elton John snubs the Dean of Perth. He says he's in a mood.'

Elton was amazed; he simply could not comprehend the Australians' pique. Everything was such a big deal, an enormous controversy. Even in the movie theaters they had a big sign flashing on the screen during the show – 'Not Suitable for Children.' It was an archaic continent, and they, the descendants of the British colonizers, seemed to despise the limey musicians who journeyed to their distant shore with their blazing electric instruments and splashy clothes. The soccer fanatic, Elton, began hoping the Australians would lose to every country, and especially Brazil. Elton was irritated.

'My cousin lives in Australia,' he told a British reporter later, 'and he had to accept the principles of a beer-drinking idiot to survive.' Of course all the pubs shut down promptly at nine and everything else had snapped closed their shutters at sundown. Australia was a nightmare for the comfort-loving piano man. The Elton John band had to play at two race tracks and a speedway in the middle of the Australian winter (summer to most of the populated world). The stage blew away on one gig and they literally played in overcoats while the rain dumped buckets of water into Elton's open piano. The band almost went mad with boredom when they weren't wrestling the elements.

'If Mary Hopkins can run into trouble there,' Elton quipped to the press later, 'well, it gives you some idea....

What they need is a tour by Led Zeppelin, the Who, and the Faces together. The country will grind to a halt.' He laughed.

Everyone involved with the world tour of 1971 would remember the Carnegie Hall gig as the culmination of the trip. Chosen by Ron Delsener, the venerable old hall, home of concert solo violinists and symphony ensembles, had magnificent acoustics, and everyone could see the stage clearly. And for an extra surprise Delsener and the group secretly spirited Sheila, his mum, across the Atlantic to see her son perform.

Elton was bowled over when, after a few seconds on stage, he glanced into the wings to see his mum, boogying and clapping her hands to the beat. By the closing chord of the final encore, tears of emotion had welled up in everyone's eyes.

'After the gig there was a tremendous celebration at the Essex House,' recalled Ron Delsener, who was the first to take EJ into the big N.Y. halls, 'with Sheila almost stealing the show from her baroque son. Sly Stone was there, and Elton wanted to meet him, so Sly came out of hiding. He hadn't worked for about a year at that time, but he came out just to meet the piano man from Pinner. He was dressed in his gold lamé suit and his huge black Afro. And Sheila loved it. And Bette [Middler] was there.'

But Elton John was flying on the crest of a wave that was moving inevitably toward a rocky shore. As it was proven in the past, Elton's strength just could not hold out. The experience had taken a drastic toll on Elton. He was on the brink of a bad nervous breakdown. 'I went to America – to Malibu – to rest and the first thing people said to me when I got off the plane was, "Hey, you're having a nervous breakdown." The news had gotten there fast. I had a glandular fever and was on the point of a crack-up. I was getting moody, shouting at people.'

'Elton was never out of commission from a musical point of view, but personality-wise he was unbearable,' admitted a close friend. 'That was the pressure of playing.'

'I mean, I've had exhaustion bouts before,' Elton added, 'but never a nervous crack-up like that.'

In the short year before, Elton had done four tours of America and one each of Japan, Australia, Europe, and England. The effort and the ego were getting to him. The power and demand of Elton's new stardom put him in the position of doing whatever he wanted to do, whenever he wanted to do it. He cut down on interviews, which were taxing because Elton was still basically shy when under the observing eye of reporters. The harder he was to get to, the more important he seemed to become. Before, he released albums on a schedule to keep interest in himself alive. Now, he held stardom in the palm of his hand. He would only release albums, in the future, when the creative call came, or when he needed more millions.

At the end of the summer of 1971, *Madman Across the Water* was released to the mercy of a press lying in ambush. Three albums in the spring had almost ruined Elton John. It was a case of appalling overkill. The American tours, the endless British gigs. No decent interval had elapsed. But, said *Melody Maker* snidely, *Madman Across the Water* will reassure those who maintained that Elton John and Bernie Taupin are endowed with more than average talent.

Once again Paul Buckmaster was allowed to shape and control the compositions which were less funky than those on *Tumbleweed*. But the arrangements and textures were more varied and interesting. 'It was an album of immense pain and intense personal statement,' commented Elton. But the heartless critics didn't care what wellsprings of sorrow and passion the songs sprang from. 'They're predictable,' opined one reviewer. 'Too easy to figure out – the intense bass and drums after the inevitable piano.'

But Elton had taken his revenge too. On 'All the Nasties' he turned his subtle musical skills to bitterly reprimand his enemies. While 'Tiny Dancer' (Bernie's tribute to his bride, Maxine) delivered like a true Los Angeles flower lyric with great lines from wordmaster Taupin, Elton's tune was diagnosed 'schizophrenic,' by the experts. 'Levon' (not Helm but one of Bernie's fictional all-American biographies about a man who was born the day the *New York Times* announced 'God is Dead') was a whopper. 'But it's obscure,' protested the pundits.

' "Razor Face," ' they said, 'was not as predictable.' Opening with excellent piano-organ tone coloring, it explored the interrelationship between an old boozer and a young one. 'Madman,' the LP's *tour de force*, was executed with a particularly relentless form of insanity; lyric and theme fulfilling function. It was a great arrangement, despite all the critics' put-downs. A six-note riff underpinned everything while Buckmaster brought in the strings in a wild, windswept tenor with echoes and tricks. The bassoon, used as one of the riff instruments, almost equaled the big horn on 'The King Is Dead.' The critics didn't complain; but ' "Indian Sunset," ' sniped the press, 'was Bernie Taupin enjoying his revival of the old West legends and reliving his youth,' while Reg was 'all togged up in warpaint and feathers.' In 'Rotten Peaches' and

'Holiday Inn,' the duo painted a picture of self-destruction.

Responded Bernie, 'It's a personal LP, especially the first side where I try to conjure up images of the past I remember. Furthermore,' he resumed vehemently. 'I think we've been the chopping block for every injustice. People say we were hyped,' he added, thinking back on the tonnage of praise heaped on the twosome which was promptly followed by the mountains of criticism. 'For God's sakes, everything is hyped to a point, and anyway what's a hype? We didn't fly journalists anywhere in a jet.' *Madman* was an album of frustration for everyone. The entire Elton troupe was going through heavy changes.

'Paul was getting . . . well, he's very strange, Paul, he can't work under pressure,' Elton stated in *Melody Maker*. 'But we were all under pressure, because we had to get the fucking album going, I don't know how that album got out.'

When they were doing the actual track of 'Madman Across the Waters,' for example, 'Paul arrived at the studio with no score. There were sixty string musicians sitting there and we had to scrap it. There were many more disasters.'

With the unleashing of *Madman Across the Water* disillusionment set in, according to one U.S. writer, 'almost perfectly proportionate to Elton's level of mass saturation. He was immediately slammed from all sides as just another singer/songwriter mistake, who couldn't throw enough live exhibitions of piano ego.'

Elton recoiled. He knew one-man shows were boring. He never wanted to do them again either. Who wants to see one guy up there on stage for two and a half hours. He knew he deserved being put down for that; he could see his critics' point. It was boring. But it was difficult to pull off a whole show with just a piano, bass, and drums. He was becoming a sort of psychedelic Ramsay Lewis.

Elton's rocket rise to stardom was unnatural, he knew it. But a lot of its unnaturalness was due to the hype of the American press. 'I love the American press,' he grimaced and blinked his soft eyes behind the rhinestone-rimmed shades he had taken to wearing. Elton was always taken in by their rave reviews. The American press never gave anyone a bad review, they'd been so intimidated by their advertisers. And Elton always believed the news when it said an album would be a success. He'd run out and buy Terry and the Teetotalers on the Garbage label, who'd been touted as a cross-pollination between the Beatles and Marvin Gaye. He'd put it on the turntable and wait for the raved-up music to curl out of the speakers. Five times out of seven he'd take it off after two cuts. He'd been hyped again. 'I always get hooked by the hype. I guess I've been hyped too. But I can understand that, and I'm prepared for the beating; everybody takes a beating if they make it.'

Elton was on the defensive, though, despite his air of bravado. 'The only thing I don't like, that really pisses me off, is when people go to concerts and review the concert – but it pisses me off when they don't get their facts right – like saying I did a bad job on "The King Must Die" when I never sang it. It's really a drag,' the irate troll declared. 'Still you have to learn to take it,' he sighed.

'For me reviews don't mean that much, they don't really sink in unless you're really sort of an avid pop maniac. You never remember them two weeks later.'

The elf with the jazzy sunglasses was getting increasingly perturbed about the superstar schizophrenia. 'I remember one incident at the Troubadour where I was actually introduced to Quincy Jones as a genius. I was so fucking embarrassed. I couldn't believe it. I apologized to him. Then I went mad at the guy, Norm Winter, who did it. Quincy Jones had come with his whole family and I was really knocked out, he must have had about eight kids. I was so mad when my press agent did that; later I told him to screw off, I'm not a superstar. But in America they tend to do that.

'But it's cooled down now. People still call me a superstar, but it's just a joke. If I were new to the business, though, and had just made my first record, I hate to think what my head would be like. The U.S.A. could destroy me with hype.' Times like those, when he was pressured, anxious, and annoyed, Elton would go on tremendous shopping sprees.

He bought dozens of shoes – from wing-tip 'toe latch' 1940s numbers to jumbo heels with gaudy designs across the toes – going berserk over the latest trendy styles to click on both sides of the Atlantic. He especially adored platform shoes and their added height. When on a shopping spree, he would buy gifts for everyone connected with the band and clothes for Sheila and his new stepfather, Fred Fairbrother, an interior decorator who loved Elton's flair for exotic paintings and bric-a-brac. And he bought glasses, hundreds of pairs of optique-art shades, granny and aviator glasses, and even wilder, calico-printed wide-rims, moongazers, owl-eyes, goggles tinted in every color of the rainbow, Mickey Mouse glasses, and palm-fronded beach specs. They came from every optician shop, thrift bin and drugstore from Bristol to San Diego. And when Elton put on a new pair it seemed that he felt an instant 'send-up' no matter who was bitching. Donning a new pair of pink bugeye shades helped him to continue his defense.

'If they like to call me a pop star, they can do it, but I know I'm a good musician. On any of our songs, they can try to figure out the basic chord sequences, and they're usually chord sequences. So let someone try to pick the chord sequences on "Your Song," for instance. I'm not a brilliant musician. I don't think I can come anywhere near Leon Russell or someone like that, but I can hold my own. I'm adequate at what I do, and I'm getting better. I can't get worse.'

About the badmouthing he was getting for his stage act, Elton replied, 'People don't know what sort of upbringing I've had. They think I'm just a moody songwriter. They say Elton John's got enough talent, he doesn't need to do that. That's nice, but they don't realize rock 'n' roll's basically where I'm at, where I was brought up. People think I'm going to be a little old man – young man – sitting at the piano à la Randy Newman and singing my soft little songs à la album,' he told *Circus* magazine. 'Right? And when I get up and kick away the piano bench, they're thinking "God, what's he doing?" They think I'm an introvert, but actually I'm just the opposite. I want to be a complete opposite of what people want me to be. I'm an extrovert when it comes to doing things like that. That sort of thing at the end of the act really knocks me out. I like building the act. What I do is start off just on piano, then I do a fast number, slow number – build it up till it's like an orgasm, really.

'And at the end, I'm all excited and I have to do it. I

just couldn't sit at the piano every night and just play soft songs. I'd get bored to bloody tears. It's not me. I've got to be performing – for about three years I intend to have a good time.

'I don't want to be taken too seriously,' he continued, lifting his shades and peering out. How many times was the piano player to say that? Over and over in one interview after another, 'Don't take me too seriously.' Why? 'Because then I won't be able to have fun with my music.'

Why is fun so important? Was it to recapture a lost childhood? Was it a defense, just in case people really don't take him seriously enough? Was it a defense against the hype and the overnight success which threw tons of pressure on him, the kind of pressure that causes some stars to run to sexual experimentation, snorting dope, shooting up, popping weird religions and seeking gurus hiding in the hills – anything to escape the hype of millions of folks who are expecting something out of them? It was a question of reality and identity. And perhaps for Elton John it was at last beginning to solve itself.

CHAPTER 11

Somewhere around the time he cut *Honky Chateau*, Elton John suddenly got younger. About ten years younger. It was as if the danger cloud lifted. The pain vanished, and he was left a prepubescent superstar who had forgotten to play grown-up. Nothing was more important than having a good time. And *Honky Chateau*, the pop LP, was simply a reflection of the positive vibrations Elton John began to have every day of his life.

He began to see that nothing in life should be taken that seriously, even music. Pop music was basically irrelevant too, in the sense that a hundred years from now people wouldn't be listening to what songs constantly flowed across the airwaves from month to month. Pop music was simply fun. And Elton John discovered that he loved fun, he loved pop music, it was his whole life. And for Elton, life was on an elite basis. He could think about his rock 'n' roll philosophy while his Rolls Royce cruised smoothly down the tree-dappled road with their stone fences running alongside.

About forty-five minutes outside London his car was sweeping through the rolling countryside in the Wentworth section of Surrey. Nosing around the curves in the stone-fence lined roads, the car made a sudden turn down a tree-lined driveway. The car headed toward an impressive, rambling, modern Beverly Hills mini-castle, Elton John's home. Parked behind white birch trees on the circular driveway were several powerful-looking autos. And from a distance one could see people dragging suitcases and musical equipment from the house and packing it in the spacious trunks of the cars.

Moving closer to the house, it was possible to see what may be one of the most sumptuous bachelor pads in England. Near the door stood a bear-sized Steiff panda worth five hundred dollars, flown in from FAO Schwarz in New York. High-ceilinged rooms of stone, wood and glass contained enormous gilded mirrors straight out of *Grand Hotel*, lots of buttoned leather furniture, low heavy tables, and two nine-foot-long sofas. There were banks of sound, visual, and electronic equipment boxed in black perspex sitting on thickly carpeted floors and underfoot everywhere were records, records, records. There were five thousand albums, twenty-five hundred 45s, sixty 78s, five-hundred eight-track cartridges and three hundred cassettes. In the corner was a mammoth grand piano.

Through the french doors a couple of gardeners could be seen scooping leaves out of the curving swimming pool. 'That pool is too hot,' Katharine Hepburn always said, when she came bicycling over for a late-afternoon swim.

Suddenly, into sight came a slight blond figure dressed in a multicolor T-shirt and blue jeans with badges pinned over every square inch of available material. The little figure looked like a button turtle just crawled out of a button-encrusted sea. He stopped and said something funny to the gardeners and hurried up the path to the house. 'We've got to get a move on it,' Elton yelled. 'The plane leaves this afternoon for Paris. It's Honky Chateau, here we come.'

The Honky Chateau adventure began when Elton's lawyer was scanning the blond troll's tax forms. For financial reasons, the solicitor decided that Elton had better start recording outside the country.

Elton, however, was perfectly content to cut his tracks at the homey Trident studios. And he thought the lawyer was joking about the tax problems until the lawyer came over and showed him the mounting bills and government forms. He wasn't joking, and Elton began to search for a foreign studio. 'I'll only go if we can find someplace peaceful without any interruptions,' he declared.

The troupe started collecting dossiers on all European studios, and one day a leaflet came through on 'this chateau.' 'It looks good,' they commented as they read about the sixteenth-century manor located forty kilometers outside of Paris. It was situated in the French countryside, in the middle of nowhere. On the grounds were a swimming pool and tennis courts – all the comforts of home. Elton's management booked time, and they prepared to make the pilgrimage.

Elton could feel that life was about to give him a new start. He had had more slags thrown at him by the press in the last month than anyone else in rock 'n' roll, but it seemed that the fourth estate had finished kicking him around. At the last minute the gang jumped in the waiting limousine; and as Elton watched the countryside slip by, his face screwed up in thoughtful reflection, he smiled as he thought about the luxurious chateau awaiting him.

The Chateau d'Herouville, hidden behind gnarled chestnut trees and thick stone walls was more elegant than he had imagined. With four separate sixteen-and thirty-two-track studios, complete with self-contained apartments and living quarters, it was a highly sophisticated recording commune. It was like the Camelot of the recording studios and, one would think, the ideal place to cut an album. Elton took a long look at the magnificent architecture through his yellow-tinted specs and in less than five-eighths of a second let out a whoop.

The entire gang piled out of the cars and ran up the driveway. 'The atmosphere's fantastic,' one shouted. 'It's a sort of luxury camp-out where everything you can think of is at our disposal, not only technical apparatus, but the living accommodations.' They all had beautiful apartments, entirely decorated in antiques. In the main hall there was a huge chandelier hanging over their heads.

'I had vowed I'd never work in France again,' Elton remembered then, thinking back to the MIDEM insult. 'We had three other very bad experiences in a row there, and that was enough. I mean they're so bloody disorganized and amateurish, just like Germany, and I really don't want to do any more public appearances in places where nobody knows what the hell they're doing. But this deal came up and we thought we'd give it a try. We heard a lot of good things about the studio – I think the Grateful Dead were the first to use it, then Pink Floyd and T Rex. What do we have to lose?'

Elton and Bernie arrived at D'Herouville with only two songs ready to cut. But the minute they arrived at the lovely French chateau the muses descended, and it all started to happen like magic. Bernie ran up and down from his little office spieling out the lyrics and Elton picked melodies right out on the piano with the lyrics right there, and everything was put together as complete arrangements.

There were about twenty of them – the group, engineers, wives, kids and all – they ate together at a long refectory table like happy monks in a funky rock 'n' roll monastery. They gorged on fabulous French food and drank vintage wines from the chateau's own vineyards. It was like an enchanted kingdom.

'But when we wanted to work, there was enough room for everybody to disappear,' added Elton. 'And each of the studios is the same. The only time you needed to see someone was out at the swimming pool.

'Anyway, it was so good, so productive, that we wrote nine songs in three days. It was just like a Motown hit factory. We were reeling them out. We rehearsed and polished for another eight or nine days, recorded in ten, and the whole thing was finished in three weeks. Unbelievable, but we were very happy with it, and I keep saying I think it's the best thing we've ever done.'

There was a much more bluesy laid-back feeling in *Chateau* than in anything they'd ever done before. 'You can feel it, especially in "Amy" and "Mellow," said Elton, now wearing green shades with canary-feathered rims. Sort of a tribute to the great French blues artists that few people know all that much about, like John Luc Ponty. 'All in all, the album was a dramatic change for the better.

'And the fact that it was done so quickly and turned out so well is another change,' Elton commented. 'It's unusual for us to do an album from the beginning of the writing to the finished product in such a short time. Normally they take a great deal of time to perfect; twelve or thirteen takes on the recording just to get it right; and it has to be as perfect as possible, doesn't it?'

He bounced up, now and then striding across the ornate French drawing room to adjust the volume on the stereo (from loud to louder) or to pour some more coffee, and then slumped back to an almost horizontal position.

The orange Texas sweat shirt, the black-velveted legs, and the stilt-heeled silver boots looked right at home. When he emphasized a point, he tended to wave his hands and stubby fingers around. They were not the long elegant digits one normally, if erroneously, associates with a master pianist, but short, thick, strong fingers as capable of pounding out a steady driving beat as of gently running up and down a melodic keyboard.

Elton really wanted *Honky Chateau* to be different. He decided not to use the heavy string arrangement of the *Elton John* LP. It would be just him and the band. It was going to be a fun album, a happier collection of songs.

They all loved the chateau, too, something about the quiet grace and elegance of the place made composing, writing, and recording a natural thing to do. Elton's mental health veered away from the crack-up zone in the mild sunshine. He luxuriated for weeks there because, actually, there was no place else to go. He couldn't escape to London and its frantic social life, which he'd have been tempted to do had he been staying in the Surrey countryside. There were no phone calls because the French phone system was so bad. They were just isolated there in the midst of one of the most civilized countries in the world.

After the slamming Elton took from the critics in 1971, it was a miracle that the mild-mannered superstar ever dared to show his face in public again. But show his face he did, first by sending *Madman Across the Water* sizzling to the top of the American charts, even while he was recording at the chateau. Then he braved the world by releasing *Honky Chateau*. Then, by casting aside his heavy mantle of string accompaniment, he revealed the semi-naked music underneath – clothed only in the G-strings of the drums, piano, bass – of the new guitarist. It was the first contribution of Davey Johnstone.

Honky Chateau, named in honor of the beautiful Chateau D'Herouville, soared to the top of the music charts to become the smash LP hit of 1972. The album actually toppled the Rolling Stones from the No. 1 spot on the charts in only the three weeks after its release. Without the string orchestration of Paul Buckmaster, the songs on *Honky Chateau* sounded less contrived. Lyrically, the album was more lucid and, rhythmically, it was one hundred times more up-beat than even *Tumbleweed Connection*. *Honky Chateau* rivaled *Elton John* as his best LP to date.

'Honky Chateau,' the title track, opened the album with more bounce to the ounce, as the piano posed counterpoint to some brass jives. Then Elton moved into the blues 'Mellow,' a lovely, clear statement of real contentment, one of the most honest happy-blues lyrics in rock and rhythm. 'I Think I'm Gonna Kill Myself,' was an ironic song, filled with a rollicking music-hall ambience and was far from the real suicidal broodings of earlier ballads. 'Rocket Man' was an example of Bernie Taupin and Elton John working together at their best, with the fantasy of outer-space travel matched by the melodic and arrangement lines. The album also had lots of simple boogie, such as 'Susie,' which reminded one of 'Susie Q.' and 'Little Susie' of another era, and the closing cut, the all-time classic, 'Hercules.' It became a pet name; even his house at Virginia Water was to be dubbed 'Hercules,' and a giant tomb like stone was placed in the front yard, carved with the letters H-E-R-C-U-L-E-S-.

'A cat named Hercules.' Elton Reg Dwight Hercules John had at last found his true identity as the Herculean pop star of the seventies.

CHAPTER 12

As he watched *Honky Chateau* head directly for the No. 1 target, Elton John vowed it was the beginning of a new era. 'There had been a sticky patch,' he admitted, as he explained the success of his new album. 'You can relate to it on stage. I knew they wouldn't be able to say, "Well, it's Elton John and his screechy orchestra."

'Bernie and I are writing so extrovertedly now. I'm also writing much more quickly for the next album.' It was June, 1972, and Elton was already embarked on his next record project.

By this time the next LP, *Don't Shoot Me – I'm Only the Piano Player*, hit the record stores. Guitarist Davey Johnstone, former Magna Carta ace, was a full-fledged member of Elton's band, and Elton began to attribute his recent bursts of creative energy to his new ax man.

'I think if we hadn't gotten Davey, the band would have broken up. I really wanted to retire. Too much attention was being focused on me. I'd been lead instrument, rhythm, instrument and voice. With no lead guitar . . . I was having to play the same thing; we'd gone as far as we could go. Now we've spread out. Gotten fuller effects.'

Yet if the press was satisfied with his new release, Elton was less proud of it than most of his previous albums. *Don't Shoot Me* was named in honor of the classic François Truffaut film *Shoot the Piano Player* in which a honky-tonk entertainer meets a tragic existential end. Although the results of the LP were happier than the flick. Elton had his reservations.

'I've lived with this album,' Elton said. 'It's got more balls. I haven't really got the voice to sing ballsy songs. I love to stand there and scream. This is more of a band album. It's better than just Elton John and his damned piano,' he told *Melody Maker*.

Elton's final comment on *Piano Player*? 'It's a disposable album.'

One fast-moving cut, 'I'm Gonna Be a Teenage Idol,' Elton dedicated to the tousle-haired matinee rocker, Marc Bolan, the lead singer of the much-put-down Tyrannosaurus Rex. 'Gonna Be a Teenage Idol,' captured the prancing singer in a rollicking whirl of seventies pop.

> Well it makes me laugh, Lord, it makes
> me cry
> And I think for once let me just get high.
> Let me get electric, put a silk suit on,
> Turn my old guitar into a tommy gun
> and root, toot shoot myself to fame
> Every kid alive gonna know my name
> An overnight phenomenon, like there's
> never been
> A motivated supersonic king of the scene . . .

It was Marc's story and Elton could identify with it. But some folks wondered why Elton would dedicate it to Marc Bolan. Elton had a perfect explanation.

On an early press release back in 1970, Elton had stated quite openly that he detested pretentious groups like Tyrannosaurus Rex. But such statements seldom go without repercussion. One day the blond bomber was browsing through a London record shop when he ran headlong into the glittering leader of T-Rex. Bolan challenged Elton on the statement to the press and Elton was so embarrassed he blushed and stammered.

When he got home he decided to make a peace offering. A Christmas present. But what could a superstar millionaire such as Marc Bolan want for Christmas? In a sudden brainstorm Elton shipped him a lifesize picture of himself with a dartboard where Elton's head should be. Not to be outdone, on Elton's birthday in March, Bolan sent the piano man a twenty-seven foot blow-up of himself which arrived Chez Hercules in a big van, plus the silver record for 'Jeepster,' Marc's hit single.

Elton's friendship with Marc began to wax so strong, in fact, that one newspaper reported defending Marc against the likes of David Bowie who had come for a gentleman's luncheon with Elton at his mansion. 'I'd always stick up for Marc – I like him,' Elton eventually admitted.

It was out of this friendship that Elton made his film debut – a three-minute cameo in the pop film *Born to Boogie*.

One day Marc Bolan called up: 'Could you just come down and we're gonna just do "Tutti Frutti" and a couple of things? It'll be fun.'

Even though Elton hated films and everyone involved with them, he went down to the studios where Ringo was shooting the rock star studded movie. 'It was nice,' Elton agreed. 'I met Ringo. All we really did was play for four hours, we didn't pose or anything. They must have lots of stuff they didn't use. Like I've said before, in that flick I look like a fuckin' gorilla. So ugly.'

But *Born to Boogie* was not the end of the camera-shy pop star's film career. Bryan Forbes, a fine film maker and Elton's neighbor, asked if he could capture the elfin's daily life on celluloid. 'It's something I've wanted to do for a long time,' the film maker pleaded, fascinated by Elton's flashy show-biz image. 'In four frenetic years,' Forbes later commented, 'Elton has come from total obscurity to three Rolls Royces in the garage of a mansion called Hercules. He's an enigma. Now possessing no inhibitions . . . totally uninhibited. Arrogant, contrite . . . the genuine article.'

Elton, along with Bernie, agreed – if they could title the flick *Elton John and Bernie Taupin Say Goodbye to Norma Jean and Other Things*. The dynamic duo had been getting increasingly involved in a new fantasy – Hollywood movies, especially the pre-1960s masterpieces. Their own movie, though, was going to be of the 'in-process' genre, cinema verité. Bryan planned to show Bernie writing a song, Elton writing the music, recording it, and playing it on stage. 'It's not going to be one of those boring films where all they show is the star lighting cigarettes,' Elton remarked, as he rocked back and forth in his deck chair while toy ducks drifted by in his tranquil swimming pool. 'I mean,' he joked, 'he's shot me in the bath.'

It was next to impossible for the determined Forbes to keep up the whirling-dervish pace Elton found to be his natural cruising speed. After releasing *Don't Shoot Me*, Elton flew off to Los Angeles to prepare for his next sonic cyclone U.S. tour. Elton wanted to check out all the old film studios, delving into the realities behind his childhood fantasies – Doris Day, Bette Davis, Roy Rogers, Hopalong Cassidy. The names were magic to Elton and Bernie. Bryan Forbes was to follow them with his camera. But imagine the dismay when the film maker descended from his jet at the L.A. airport to find that a crowd had been attracted by a huge motorcoach on which was written in enormous flashy colors the sign: 'Welcome Ernest Thrush, World's Greatest Singer.' Elton contrived to make the fans believe Bryan was 'Ernest' and the distinguished actor-director was promptly torn to pieces by celebrity-hungry fans.

Prowling about L.A. was fine with Elton, for a while, but soon a familiar itch began to drive the tiny celebrity to the big concert halls in search of that certain kind of excitement only a big show can arouse. He crept out one night to see the Alice Cooper show at the Hollywood Bowl. It was an incredible experience for Elton. The helicopters overhead, dropping thousands of panties, the fireworks, the stage shenanigans. It was the best-produced show he'd ever seen. He was amazed at Alice, like the rest of the Cooper fans.

'I was caught up in it myself, scrambling for a pair of panties! And his band was so tight! You can't do that back in the U.K.,' he might have thought. 'You'd get the job's worths backstage saying, "You can't do that, who's going to clean up the mess?"'

Touring fever was heating up the zany little pop star and he immediately went into a huddle with the entire gang to map strategy. Later that spring, Elton announced a ten-week, forty-five-city cyclone-powered U.S. tour to begin in September 1972. It was a juggernaut which promised to be one of the most ambitious tours in the history of rock 'n' roll.

It was the record-breaking series which came to be known throughout the world as the 'Legs Larry Tour' because of the wild antics of the tap-dancing ex-Bonzo Doo Dah man. The tour began in Los Angeles and seared its way eastward, driving the audiences bananas with glee at every performance.

In the middle of this spectacular mission, however, Elton John received an important summons. At the request of H.R.H. Queen Elizabeth II, the pudgy pumper was to appear for her Royal Variety Performance in London on October 30, 1972.

Elton gasped when he received the formal request. He, Elton Hercules Dwight, was to be the first rocker since the godlike Beatles to receive such an exalted invitation – a command performance!

Waving good-bye and blowing kisses to most of his entourage, Elton and the band took off from a flat Oklahoma landscape on October 28 and winged their way to London. Elton's fat (but thinning) body shook and shivered with fear at the prospect of playing before the Queen herself – plus the fact Elton was co-billed to play with none other than that prototypical lamé-garbed ivory tickler, Liberace.

When the august body of patrons assembled and as the Queen settled herself to view the spectacle, Elton took a deep breath. Liberace was to appear first, and Elton thought he would burst before the middle-aged showman finished his set. But he did and was great. It was said later, in fact, that Liberace was the only decent act on the bill.

Elton finally went on stage before the Queen and the audience – the ultimate in stuffed shirts. He had two numbers to do, and the crowd kept calling stiffly: 'Do "Your Song," ' or 'do "Rocket Man." ' But the mischievous piano man brought out Legs Larry to tap dance to 'I Think I'm

Gonna Kill Myself,' and the band released balloons that actually made farting noises. The entire effect was lost on TV, but the audience was shocked and infuriated as the balloons whizzed around, going pffft, pffft, all around their tiaraed heads while they murmured 'Ooooooo! Oooooooo!' Backstage the roadies and friends were rolling on the floor in uncontrollable belly laughter.

On November 1, Elton rejoined his traveling band in Tulsa, Oklahoma, where they waited excitedly to hear the story of the command performance. They laughed merrily as Elton recounted the story of the farting balloons and told them of how Liberace continued to wheel in trunks of clothes while all the stuffed shirts badgered him for autographs.

'That show was probably the culmination,' reminisced Elton's American promoter, Ron Delsener. 'But then again probably not. Because Elton likes to do something different all the time. He's such a visual performer, he doesn't need anything but himself. But he likes to surprise people; he's full of fun. At Carnegie Hall he used dancing girls. It was very Busby Berkeley – he used girls from L.A. and New York dancing schools, and a choreographer was hired to teach him dance steps. His girls came out in black and white sequined costumes; and they had these wigs,' Ron looped his arms around his sandy hair, 'indicative of the early forties and they all looked exactly alike, like Kewpie dolls.

'Bernie usually came out at the end of the show. And Marv Tabolsky, Elton's road manager, he dresses up like Liberace and pretends he's playing the piano. Who knows where Elton comes up with all these ideas. He stages his own show. After the show I might say, well, next year let's do this and that, but basically he put everything together himself. He's very inventive. He's probably one of the brightest . . .' Ron drifts off in thought. 'There's a lotta bright guys in this business – but he's one of the brightest guys I've met.'

'Elton has perfect taste in everything he does. He's pretty aware of what's going on, not just in the music business but in the world. Gourmet, you know. He knows good wines, he knows fine art. He's versed in most subjects. So, anyone who's got some background in taste will know when he performs – works as well as plays – he's gonna perform with a certain finesse.' Ron waved his checker-clothed arm with a flourish. 'A certain flair. He knows how to please a crowd, how to get them excited. Using these things – gimmicks, stage effects, whatever you call them, even his eyeglasses (one pair he had made up for five thousand dollars) – the kids get off on that. Next year he'll do something entirely different. He picks up a magazine or he sees a Groucho Marx movie and starts playing Groucho.

'Yeah, Elton's a real entertainer. Before this, in the sixties we didn't have entertaining acts. We just had recording acts. Just people who'd sit up there with their guitar and head hanging down not talking to anyone. They come out there, play their guitar and split without saying a word or generating excitement. But Elton generates something through his music and through his personality.'

A party of reporters set off one bright spring day to pay a visit to Elton John at his palatial digs, Chez Hercules. A clutch of press people headed down the circuitous route from London, across the chalk downs, forests and farmland that lie to the southwest of the Cromwell Road extension. Elton John was not intent on adopting the secrecy of a Howard Hughes, even though a busload of fans had the week before pulled up at the local police station, demanding to know the direction to his home.

Turning down the wood-lined road, the pen-pushing crowd set their sights on the tidy jewellike pad, situated among a warren of discreetly screened villas. A spacious Rolls Royce Phantom limousine sat in the driveway, flanked by a Bentley and a Ferrari. The gardens around the house were immaculately manicured. Beyond the edge of the shrubs could be seen the rising construction of a new house, big enough to enclose the expanding thousands of records, paintings, and other objects which threatened to burst Hercules at its seams.

Inside, there was little clutter in the living room. Beautiful objects were enhanced by lighting, setting, and space. The suit of armor guarding the stairway gleamed with care and the marble bathroom – the most expensive in the world, according to its builders, Wimpey's of London – was a picture of tidy perfection. The bath had an enormous tub specially equipped with a rubber headrest. And the towels were placed in orderly stacks.

'This makes the *House and Garden* [Pick of the Month] seem like a Quonset hut,' quipped one guest as he gazed at an original Andy Warhol silkscreen, one of the 'Electric Chair' series.

Not a square inch of wall space was unoccupied. 'Elton digs paintings by an elegantly coiffed friend of the star's,' informed the press, pointing to a Grandma Moses-type oil painting that hung over one of the nine-foot-long leather-upholstered sofas. 'Emily is all the rage among rock stars here,' the woman continued, her elegant features profiled against the landscapes and abstracts which covered the walls. 'But Emily adores Elton. He has over forty of her paintings while George Harrison has only nine. This one over the couch is the biggest Emily in existence. Harrison was dying for it, but Emily said she would only sell it to Elton.

'Bryan Forbes lives on that side,' she gestured to Elton's nearest neighbor, 'while on the right is the house where his mum, Sheila Fairbrother lives with Fred. Sheila may well be the most important friend Elton has,' the smartly dressed woman continued, enjoying the attention she was getting from the open-mouthed throng. 'She's very attractive, very modern, doesn't look her age, and is in a particular semielegant way, very smartly dressed. She loves a good time. She also oversees Elton's house when he's flying all over the world.

'Fred Fairbrother, her husband, was an interior decorator. Now he's almost retired except for helping Elton with his decorating. Fred's a barrel of laughs.' The woman stopped and chuckled as she thought of some of Fred's high jinx. 'He loves to wear Saint Laurent clothes. When he goes to Beverly Hills he stays at the Beverly Hills' Bungalows, those semimansions by the coast. Fred's very hip; nothing too outrageous, there's never a situation where he or Sheila feel uncomfortable. They pick up on anything.'

The gang headed up to Elton's game room. Apart from his swimming pool, this room promised to be the most amusing. The reporters ran around like delighted children, plugging coins in the real juke box stocked by Elton with hits by Judge Dread, Rod Stewart, and T-Rex. They played a round at the three-hundred-dollar backgammon set, a twenty-pointer of table tennis, and a session each at the slot machine, golf putter, and hockey. The room was lit by a giant Hercules sign, on the base of which was inscribed 'To a swell guy,' and signed Maxine and Bernie. It had been a birthday gift. There were hundreds of other games.

Upstairs in Elton's vast closet were his fifty pairs of platform heels in every height and design imaginable; and hundreds of suits, T-shirts, and trousers lined his cavernous closet, shimmering in the ubiquitous glitter and lamé.

'I'm planning to drop the glitter,' a voice suddenly popped into the room, and everyone spun around to see the man himself.

'Those shiny ones are going. I'm having a designer design a whole lot more for me now because I'm bored with those tall suits. I've had them for ages. There are no limits to what I can wear on stage.' The gang trouped back to the living room where Sheila suddenly emerged in an Elton John T-shirt, bearing tea and cakes.

'When he first started wearing all that way-out gear,' she laughed, 'I was worried about being seen with him on the street. But you get used to everything in the end.'

Yet, amid all the splendor, there was one possession that gave Elton supreme pleasure: his suitcase full of spectacles. The last time he was in L.A. he had twenty-five pairs of sunglasses made to order at a custom shop where one could get anything to see out of for a price. He had a pair fashioned with an ELTON written on them that flashed on and off. And he bought a pair with battery-charged wipers that swished back and forth across the tinted lenses.

He got them at every optical shop in every town across the U.S.A. But his favorite was a little place in Hollywood that made them especially with Elton in mind. They thought he was insane, but they made them just the same. His specs are not just for show, for without them Elton John could not see beyond the end of his grand piano.

That piano, big and black, occupied one corner of the main lounge, and Elton swore he never played his own compositions on it but just used the instrument for doodling purposes. He stopped writing when he came home. With *Don't Shoot Me* and the new one, *Goodbye Yellow Brick Road*, he wrote the tunes entirely within the acoustically tiled studio. He'd sit down at the piano with the lyrics they'd brought down from upstairs and the band would come around in a little while to pick up the compositions. It was almost unbelievable – in Jamaica, Elton wrote twenty-five songs in three days.

'In a lot of ways it's frustrating to be tied to the piano,' Elton admitted to *Creem* magazine with slightly more chagrin than his smile would indicate, 'because you can't do much with it. I guess I've always been a frustrated guitarist, and it's a tremendous sensation just to play three chords. I can play about four chords on a good day.'

The superstar picked up a shiny new Les Paul and hooked it up to an amp and stood there, like a small warthog, blasting away. He played the riff over and over again while the sun went down behind the white, aspen-lined driveway. He played the chord, listened, and freaked out on the feedback.

Often he dreamed of being a wild ax crasher like Pete Townshend of the Who, or James Williamson of the

Stooges. There was always an aura clinging to them as they bashed out the chords. What a thrill, what a release to be able to leap across the stage, strings twanging, guitar gleaming in the spotlights.

But then again he often thought he wanted to compose a downer type of album. He wanted to get caught up in other lives and other identities. A suicide album because he enjoyed listening to depressing music. That's why he liked Leonard Cohen so much, because Cohen always depressed him, and he really enjoyed it. He felt that everybody needed to listen to depressing music once in awhile.

Elton broke out of his reverie and ordered Dom Perignon for his guests. No sooner had it arrived and been poured than a guest promptly spilled it all over the carpet. The guests sat and watched as Elton sponged down the hand-embroidered rug (delivered by messenger from the Middle East after a hair-raising overland passage of seven weeks) with quiet resignation. The guest was mortified, and Elton tried to erase the embarrassment with reassurances that it was, actually, perfectly all right.

Elton squeezed out the champagne and rubbed more vigorously. He was used to such accidents. All the newspapers had reported his 250-guest Christmas party of the season before, a party complete with female impersonators and strippers.

At that time Donovan, too, was planning a bash, and it was reported that he'd invited the whole world. Keith Moon had been invited, but said that he'd only come if it was a booze-up. No fairy dust for him. Rod Stewart, also a neighbor to Donovan and Elton, had accepted, provided there were more than mushrooms and toadstools.

Admitting that rock stars don't always make the best neighbors, Elton told one English reporter that he'd actually had trouble insuring his house because he lived too near the wildman, Keith Moon.

'I was going to buy another house too,' he quipped, 'called Charters Farm. When I called the owner, I called it Farter's Charm... by mistake, of course.'

The sun had completely set beyond the swimming pool. Elton drew the many yards of drapes across the picture window and switched on the multicolored ball of glass finds, and asked the guests if they had heard the funniest, saddest, and most excruciating tape ever recorded — the legendary Troggs tape.

The tape was made while the Troggs were recording their next single. The engineer left the tape running and since then everybody had been demanding a copy.

The reporters listened to the Troggs as Elton explained the hit group of some six years ago, struggling to communicate with each other through a melee of oaths, broad English dialects, and missed drum beats. It was calculated that a certain four-letter word was used nearly 138 times in about ten minutes.

The tape was enough to drive away even the heartiest, and soon, after everyone's champagne glasses had been tipped and drained, the press party bid the tiny gentleman adieu and left Elton John dancing to the bouncy beat of Stevie Wonder's 'Superstition.'

CHAPTER 13

'If you're going bald like me, then try . . .' said Elton, advertising hair restorer on station KMET in Los Angeles in November, 1973. Elton, who was manning the mikes like a hairless but elderly baby, took over the Richard Kimball show on KMET for a couple of hours, picking out his own records, reading the ads, and generally horsing around.

'It's EJ the DJ,' he announced when the show went on the air live, following a news broadcast that included a warning about dangerous waterbeds – about leaks and singed rubber.

Elton's selection of music included Ike and Tina Turner, Bowie, Ringo, Anne Peebles, Mott the Hot, Robin Trower, Jackson Browne, John Lennon, Loudon Waineright III, Jimmy Cliff, Hudson, Dave Mason, Graham Nash, Iggy and the Stooges, and the Stones.

Among other things he did an ad for the Troubadour in L.A. 'I started out at the Troubadour,' he gurgled, 'and look where it got me – a forty-five-dollar-a-day job as a dee-jay on KMET.'

'Elton has always maintained that everything is disposable,' said Eric Van Lustbader, 'and that is true for him. There are so many facets of his personality it would take thirteen stories to capture just a part of his character. He gets into things very deeply, but they're short term. He gets bored with them and abandons them if there's any trouble. With long-term projects he gets bored midway through and says he wants to go to something else. That's the way he is. He's got so much energy it's hard for him to tie it into any one thing. The exception is Rocket Records, though, to which he's devoting an incredible amount of energy. Especially to Kiki Dee, an artist on Rocket Records whose album is terrific. He picked her up – well, she's been around awhile. Elton produced her LP. It's unusually difficult for a musician to think like a producer; musicians tend not to hear the overall sound of a cut. But Elton can do this.'

The idea for Rocket Records came to them when Elton and the band were staying at the Chateau D'Herouville for the second time. One night the group of Elton people were sitting around the giant wooden refectory table in the chateau's dining room, where so many other brainstorms of the group's had whipped fantasy into reality. Davey Johnstone, the guitarist who'd become an official member of the band, was planning to cut his own album. 'But,' explained Elton to the others, 'he doesn't have a label to go out on.'

Elton had gone to a number of record companies, both British and American, he related, but nobody would give Davey a reasonable deal.

'So what are we going to do?' asked a band member, pouring himself another goblet of the chateau's own vintage wine. 'Well,' started Elton, who was finishing his umpteenth goblet of the brilliant amber wine. 'Ah, let's start our own label.'

'And after hearing Davey's album, which has taken a year to get together, not for lack of material, but because he hasn't had time in the studio, those people are really going to be kicking themselves, because it's a fucking masterful album,' Elton declared.

'But that's how it started. The few of us involved, Bernie and I, Steve Brown who handles A&R side, John Reid, who will basically handle the business, and we just set out to cultivate new talent.'

But the fantasy didn't transform itself into a real record company by magic. For a while it seemed as if the crew preferred the pipe dream to remain in the tobacco pouch of their imaginations. It took the power of a song to kick Elton John into action. That song was the opening cut of Elton's album *Don't Shoot Me – I'm Only the Piano Player*.

It was December, 1971. Kids from Baltimore to Newcastle were rockin' 'n' boppin' to the 'Crocodile Rock' single Elton had released from the *Don't Shoot Me* album. It was a hot, jivin', catchy tune and it was predictably gobbling its way up the charts. But meanwhile Elton was desperately struggling to get a mellower song out from under the stubborn thumb of the Dick James record company. And Elton was worried that 'Daniel,' the touching tribute to a friend, would never get released at all. Dick, still Elton's manager and publisher, firmly believed the track had no commercial appeal and would harm the LP sales and compete with the smash hit 'Crocodile.' The record bigwigs at Dick James Music tried in vain to convince the fiery pianist to select a more upbeat tune as the follow-up to the million-selling beast, 'Crocodile.' But the stubby songwriter angrily sputtered, 'It's one of the best songs we've ever written. I don't care if it's a hit or not. I just want it out.'

To that comment, Dick James himself issued a rejoinder

in the form of a trade-paper interview: 'This is a very one-sided viewpoint. Let's get the facts straight,' he blustered. 'It's untrue to say that I don't like "Daniel." It's a beautiful, fantastic number, one of the best Elton and Bernie have written. And it's the first title on the album.

'Steve Brown, coordinator of Elton's sessions, Stephen James, the chief of the label, and myself all came to the same conclusion independently about not releasing "Daniel" as a single. And Elton must have some regard,' James orated in fatherly tones, 'for Steve's judgment, at least, for he has signed him as an executive for his own record company.

'We are spending seven thousand pounds on advertising the album on TV and in the trade press. We are releasing "Daniel" as a single solely because of the pressure from Elton . . . and, may I add, against the wishes of MCA, who distribute Elton's records for us in the U.S.

'As for our saying that we did not want to spend money on advertising "Daniel" when such a large amount for the album was spent, we have not reached any compromise with Elton. We understand he is still thinking about it.'

But just about two weeks after war broke out between Elton and Dick James, the piano player emerged as the winner and champion. The single was finally released, although in Britain Elton was forced into the unorthodox position of paying all the advertising costs himself.

But the cloudy tale of 'Daniel' ended with an ironically silver lining. Announced Elton sarcastically, 'Dick says he'll pay me back for the advertisements if the single makes the Top Ten. Isn't that nice?'

On January 12, 1972, the single 'Daniel' was released in the U.K. for Dick James Music. It was B-sided, perhaps for good luck, with 'Skyline Pigeon,' the early masterpiece from the *Empty Sky* album. The recut version had been arranged by Paul Buckmaster. But the 'Daniel' episode really served as the last straw between Elton and his old management. He knew he had to gain some artistic freedom. He was a rich man, after all, with his own millions to launch a label. 'If you're going to devote a lot of time to something,' he declared like a true businessman, 'you might as well own it.'

A year later, in the midst of recording and social events, Elton and his team had begun to set up the new company, Rocket Records.

MCA Records gave Elton a hefty advance, but that money more or less went into finding an office and staff. First they recruited Penny Valentine, the reviewer who'd praised *Empty Sky* (those many eons ago in 1969) so highly that Eric Van Lustbader had sent away for it. Rocket Records turned out to be a small staff – only eighteen loyal Eltonites. 'It's quite cheery, actually,' Penny said. 'We're very lucky to be surrounded with so many nice people at Rocket Records.'

Rocket couldn't start out paying fifty-thousand-dollar advances immediately, and they didn't want to, even though it meant they couldn't sign name acts. But they didn't particularly want that either. They were going to scout and find new people. They were going to give a fairer deal and a better royalty rate than most beginning and unknown groups could get from the mammoth companies and complexes such as the Warner-Elektra-Atlantic monolith. Certainly it was an idyllic plan. But it was one that sooner or later any artists who had an intelligent thought in their heads would have to arrive at – the Moody

Blues, Led Zeppelin, the Grateful Dead, and the Jefferson Airplane, as well as the Beatles had all instigated their own labels.

But Elton planned that Rocket be something different from the companies that had gone before. Elton himself was not planning to record on his own label. He thought it would dampen everyone else. He compared the Moody Blues to Trapeze, the former's little-brother act on the same label and concluded Moody Blues' presence was inhibiting to the newer act.

'I said three years ago, I'd be retired by now,' Elton said laughing in 1973. But on March 25, on Elton Reg Dwight Hercules John's 26th birthday, the blond superstar threw what may not prove to be the biggest party of his career as the Perle Mesta of rock 'n' roll, but most likely the most important.

On March 25th, Elton John launched Rocket Records in a style memorable in the annals of rock 'n' roll for years to come. It was a massive booze-up free-for-all on board the sloop *John D.* moored off the Thames embankment. 'It was the biggest name-dropping rave-up of recent times,' wrote the musical press. Rod Stewart was there clad in leopard-skin jacket sipping expensive brandy, while the rest of the Faces circled the decks. Cat Stevens appeared camouflaged behind a Captain Hook beard. The dude in the white floppy apple hat was none other than Paul Simon, looking tiny and lost. Ringo lurked in a furry freak brothers beard while Harry Nilsson flashed a pocket tape recorder the size of a candy bar. Elton cut the cake with the aid of June Bolan (without Marc) and everybody else sat round and pretended not to watch the stripper remove what little remained of her garb.

Indeed, it was voted unanimously to be the party of the year. Tony Prince, royal voice of Radio Luxembourg, was heard above the din of the others.

Patti Harrison was there (but not George nor the McCartneys).

In August a repeat performance was given in Hollywood, Elton's foster home. Held in the western town back lot of Universal Film Studios, the several old-time stores were decorated with contemporary names resembling Bernie Taupin fantasy time pieces. The gathering was an odd assortment of glitter and casual. One girl, in bold economy, wore only a short see-through dress and black bikini panties. Elton was resplendent in snazzy satin BVD shorts, white knee socks and an almost plain blue and green jacket. Both sides of his hair were dyed bright pink. Bernie was more down to earth in a white Edwardian summer suit and ruffled blouse. Maxine looked like Little Bo Peep in a huge-brimmed straw hat and padded-shouldered in a light jacket with red hearts sprinkled liberally upon it. There was a simulated gun fight after which Elton belted out on a battered out-of-tune piano old rock 'n' roll favorites – 'Whole Lotta Shakin Going On,' and the more recent classic, 'Crocodile Rock,' and 'Daniel.' And the sun sank into the Pacific.

Has Elton John changed in the last four years? 'Very little,' replied Eric Van Lustbader. 'He's more self-confident, slightly more outspoken. Before he was exceedingly shy. But what he says and does now is nothing he wouldn't have thought or wished to do before.'

And what does the elfin piano-thumper have to say?

'Basically, you are what you are. Success hasn't affected me ego-wise at all. The only drag is that you have to sort of register in hotels under different names. And you have to shut yourself away somewhat. But ego-wise it hasn't altered me a bit. I'm still the same person I always was. It's just the fact that I've become accepted. A lot of people think I'm going to be an egomaniac. But it's really nothing. I'm no better than anyone else. I do what I do quite well and I've got acceptance for it. I just go out there and have fun. That's what it's all about. I just hope the crowds have a good time. The kids are the most important thing. You gotta remember that all the time. The audience is more important than you are, because without them you'd be nowhere. I don't want to be known as just a rock 'n' roll gimmick act. I know I do all that jumping around and one of these days I'm going to topple over and go straight through the piano. The perfect ending. I'll come out in little slices underneath.'

ELTON JOHN'S
ASTROLOGICAL CONFIGURATION

Whenever he is approached about his astrological sign and influences, Elton John invariably responds half-jokingly, half-seriously, 'I was born under the dollar sign.' He draws an imaginary $ in the air. 'That's my sign.'

Arthur Gatti, astrologer and managing editor of *Astrology Guide* and *Your Personal Astrology* magazines, is plotting a solar chart for the piano-playing superstar, a chart based on his birth date and place, the exact hour of Elton's birth being unknown. Located high within the walls of the Warner-conglomerate building in New York City, Gatti's office includes a human skull grinning maniacally on his desk. The candle mounted on the skull's forehead drips tallow down the temples. It is not lit when Gatti begins to analyze the cryptic signs he has drawn on a circle divided into twelve zones.

'Elton's chart is a solar chart only, based on the sun's being the ruler of the First House, rather than having the actual birth house which it might have had under a close reading.

'The moon here is in the Second House, which is a money house. The moon placement is a Taurus placement, Taurus being a sign of the throat and of the voice. It is also the sign of artistry and accomplishment. In the house of money it indicates a lot of success, the moon also being the symbol of public popularity.

'The moon is in Taurus, as I said – the so-called "exalted place" of the moon. This indicates the maximum operation of the moon's qualities. It is also a pioneering aspect because the moon is just about thirty degrees away from the sun, which is an Aries sun, and therefore indicates a person who likes to be first in many ways. He likes to accomplish newness. This placement shows a healthy respect for the material rewards of accomplishment.'

The long-haired astrologer puts the finishing touches on his exploration of Uranus in the Third House. 'After the moon, there's this little thing that looks like a pair of earphones. It's the point where the moon crosses the northern path of the ecliptic, or the apparent path of the center of the earth. This eclipse point gives energy to the Third House, which concerns very fortunate contacts with people, good connections in the business world, good in the communicating or transporting areas of involvement with others. In foreign lands, though, the interpersonal contacts will be met with some difficulty. There may be some problems with courts, and, generally speaking, there may be the possibility of bad luck in far-away places.

'Uranus in the Third House: It indicates a suddenness of communication. Elton must have a graceful manner of expression. He's very charming. But there may be a holding back, some inhibition, and lack of spontaneous expression. It may be good or bad, depending on the situation. At times, though, he has tremendous mental grace, intellectual flare, a lot of enthusiasm, individualism, creativity springing out of everyday forms of expression.

'But there's also a great capacity for unknown wellsprings of violent expression, of explosive tendencies, maybe more out of fear than anger. It seems connected to Mars and Pisces, which are in the Twelfth House here, which is an area of worry and concern.

'There is a lot of concern for the welfare of others in this field so that Mars creates a nervous tension, creates an inner tightness and a need to hold certain things in that he's afraid will explode outward. This is especially true concerning attitudes about people close to his roots – elders, parents, relatives. There is a great deal of control over his explosive emotions. But among his peers, he relaxes and becomes more explosive and spontaneous. His inhibitions and control among parents is a sort of playback from those serious areas of his experience, probably childhood and adolescence.

'Uranus is also the media: it's the rock revolution, so to speak; also the act of exploding old forms to experiment with new things, new consciousness. There's a lot balanced between positive and negative, or strain and ease in Elton's chart. The ease comes from a natural creativity that makes him at home in these volatile areas – the artistic flair. But the innovative creativity that can produce the very new, very refreshing, also suffers from the fear of his own violence. The two planets involved are very intense ones, worrisome, disturbing of sleep, disturbing of consciousness.

'But things should begin to look up emotionally. The explosive energies have long since begun to burst out. Now they will take over the areas of joy, as the moon takes ascendancy. He's going to work out problems relating to women and love, at least. And he's going to have a lot more fun.'

It is getting dark outside; Rockefeller Plaza is shadowed in fog. Arthur Gatti lights the candle on the skull and continues his reading.

'The restricting syndrome of Saturn in the Fourth House wants Elton to behave as he behaved as a child, rather than allowing emotions to come out spontaneously. But Saturn is creative too. In the Fourth House Saturn represents the traditional core, the father. And it is counterbalanced here by the moon, which means material success and the mother. With Saturn-square-the-moon, consequently, there may be many hangups about the mother and the mother's role, insecurities about her and what she represents. Perhaps he suffered separation and loss of security while in school. Perhaps there was a disastrously scarring experience which Saturn in the Fifth House cusp indicates.

'The Fifth House is the area of enjoyment. And this ability in Elton was impeded in terms of response situations. But he has learned to overcome the Saturnian influences and to come to enjoy the far more basic things that life has to offer.

'The Fifth House is the creative house. It is the area of youth, passionate attachment, and romantic love. Saturn on the cusp brings the relationships with the father and mother into its realm. He may have had difficulty express-himself in joyful ways as a child. I would suspect that, until a teenager, he suffered some sadness about those things, such as parental relationships. He might have been very repressed. Often, too, this configuration indicates that a child's parents may have had only a functional, rather than loving, relationship during his conception and early years. That's hard to say, however.

'I see great potential, though, for Elton to continue to grow into fluid structures of expression, fixed in terms of their artistic content, but changeable in whatever way he wants to change them. Saturn is the bareness of something, while the moon is the limitlessness, the full principle, wealth, love, and the richness of life. Here the two come into conflict.

'In the actual Fifth House is Pluto. It indicates the deepest probing and self-knowledge. It is the area of control too. If a parent wields the controls, that parent needs to be exorcised to some extent. It is the area of birth. Connected to the moon with a square, it probably signifies some difficulty with women, something to do with infidelities or diversionary activities of some sort. But this is not clear: Pluto is a very weird visitor into the twentieth century.

'Neptune is located in the house of partnership,' Gatti exclaims as he bends over his compass and rules the lines straight across the diagram. 'It's a musical aspect if there ever was one! Neptune ruling Pisces.

'Neptune in the Seventh House is an incredibly musical aspect. But it upsets the balance of friendships, of partnerships and intimate relationships. According to the solar analogy in Elton's chart, impresssionability plays a large part in his friendships, also self-deception, things he wants to believe about people. But this could be useful in a sense, because Neptune is the music planet – Neptune pulls the tunes out,' (the astrologer smiles at his pun and continues) 'so that a friend will be the one to do that – inspire him, pull the tunes out. Without someone for him to reflect off of, he can't pull those things out.

'So, possibly friends are necessary for his musical creativity. And many of these friendships may be based on as much unreality as can be gained from a situation. He's liable to imagine a lot about the people he's standing on equal footing with. Perhaps the only way he can relate to his music is through another person.' Gatti hesitates.

'But it's not a natural, easy relationship, as it would be if it were in a conjunction, let's say, of the sun in the Seventh House. Then you'd say it was a very natural situation where it was easy for him to get things from other people and turn them into musical accomplishments. But here' (Gatti concentrates intently on the hieroglyphs) 'when it oppresses like this, there's something in his life where you have to say a price is being paid. There's some sorrow, self-sacrifice, pain – someone's suffering in this relationship, and at some point or another, the price's being paid without it being realized. Neptune's where something's escaped without being seen.'

The astrologer paces around his office and the candle flutters. 'Neptune is gaseous and has to do with the least tangible forces one has.

'But Elton's still young; he has these things, or he'll grow into them eventually,' Gatti goes on ambiguously. 'Eventually he'll come to grips with his psychic powers if he hasn't already realized he has them, or accepted them yet. They will always be around for him to explore. The only thing is, a lot of people with psychic powers get hooked on some kind of escape, usually chemical, from themselves, and from other connected ones, and from the power that this kind of aspect confers. They feel the depths of sudden understanding that says there's no time, for instance. It's very difficult for people with Saturn-square-the-moon, where time is always important – it sort of drops, minute by minute, in the Lunar path . . .'

The astrologer breaks off, kneading his prominent forehead with his fingertips. 'But once he learns to deal with the Neptunian aspects of his relationship with his partner, that explosive quality which has been suppressed very strongly, the, ah, artistic genius (Mercury span Pisces) may break loose with all its disturbing electricity. It may shatter what has traditionally been holding him together. Pisces is a very unknown area.'

And the star-charter returns to his calculations.

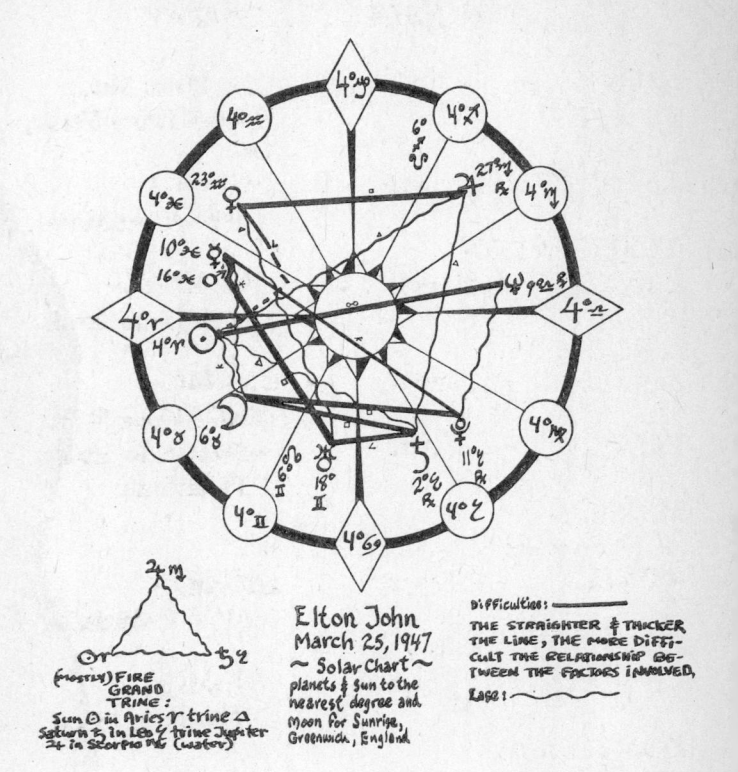

Elton John
March 25, 1947
~ Solar Chart ~
planets & sun to the nearest degree and Moon for Sunrise, Greenwich, England

(mostly) FIRE GRAND TRINE:
Sun ☉ in Aries ♈ trine △ Saturn ♄ in Leo ♌ trine Jupiter ♃ in Scorpio ♏ (water)

Difficulties: ─────
THE STRAIGHTER & THICKER THE LINE, THE MORE DIFFICULT THE RELATIONSHIP BETWEEN THE FACTORS INVOLVED.

Ease:

ELTON JOHN DISCOGRAPHY

EMPTY SKY	1969 (June)	Dick James Music © Dick James Music, Inc.
ELTON JOHN	1970	UNI-MCA © Dick James Music
TUMBLEWEED CONNECTION	1970	UNI-MCA ©Dick James Music
11-17-70	1971	UNI-MCA ©MCA Records, Inc.
FRIENDS	1971	Paramount Records © Paramount
MADMAN ACROSS THE WATER	1972	UNI-MCA ©MCA Records, Inc.
HONKY CHATEAU	1972	UNI-MCA © This Record Co.
DON'T SHOOT ME – I'M ONLY THE PIANO PLAYER	1972	UNI-MCA © This Record Co.

GOODBYE YELLOW BRICK ROAD	1974	UNI-MCA © This Record Co.
CARIBOU	1974	MCA © This Record Co.
GREATEST HITS		MCA © This Record Co.